OFFBEAT OREGON

OFFBEAT OREGON

A Connoisseur's Collection of Travel Discovery in Oregon

MIMI BELL

CHRONICLE BOOKS
San Francisco

Library of Congress Cataloging in Publication Data

Bell, Mimi.
  Offbeat Oregon.

  1. Oregon — Description and travel — 1981-   — Guidebooks. I. Title.
F874.3.B44   1983   917.95'0443   83-5229
ISBN 0-87701-274-1

Editing: Linda Gunnarson

Book and cover design: Diana Fairbanks

Composition: Diana Fairbanks

Cover photograph: Anne Hinds

Photo credits: Oregon Department of Transportation, pages 1, 7, 12, 70, 72, 75, and 121; Marje Blood, Eugene, pages 8 and 10; Elizabeth Brooke Smith, Eugene, pages 33 and 36; Geoff Parks, Portland, page 51; Oregon State Highway Travel Section, page 53; Medford *Mail Tribune,* page 66; all other photographs by Mimi Bell.

Chronicle Books
870 Market Street
San Francisco, California 94102

CONTENTS

FOREWORD

Offbeat Oregon is geared to the *serendipities* of Oregon travel rather than to the *spectaculars* (although the two overlap frequently). Knowing the Columbia Gorge and Crater Lake and 32,000 acres of Sand Dunes can speak for themselves eloquently, Mimi Bell has chosen, for the most part, to sing the praises of the quieter, but no less entrancing, "small wonders" with which the state is blessed.

Starting in the Astoria area where Oregon's history began, she guides her readers to the multitude of fascinating artifacts that confirm the records of discovery and settlement. Then, swiftly, she entices them along the magic roller coaster highway which borders the state's western edge to explore one of its imposing promontories, the "smallest navigable harbor in the world," a haunted lighthouse, and a floating museum or two; pausing now and then to sample the wares of special small restaurants and intriguing shops. (And yes, she does overlap a bit, for an overview of Oregon's Sahara by the sea.)

She shunpikes north as far as Salem in the Willamette Valley, renewing acquaintance with historic Brownsville; enjoying side trips to visit a llama farm near Albany and to attend a whistler's festival/contest in Corvallis.

Swinging south again she investigates more surviving villages of an earlier era, Oakland and Jacksonville and Glide, stopping here and there to sample delicious delicacies made famous by word-of-mouth advertising by delighted customers, Mexia's homemade pies, for instance, baked as needed and always slightly warm from the oven.

The colorful theme tying the sections together like a bright blue ribbon is her love affair with the birds and wildflowers she discovers wherever she goes. Daisies and foxgloves and Queen Anne's Lace; yarrow and Scotch broom, wild lilacs and flowering currant are among the first of the vast variety of blooms she "gathers" for her memorial bouquet as she explores the crazy-quilt pastoral landscapes bordered by the meandering back roads she wanders.

A brief tour of the little town named for the "triumverate of local peaks" (The Three Sisters), and she's taking to the road again, heading into sagebrush country which segues into desert, once the bed of an ancient inland sea, "inhabited" now by ghost towns and the fossils of animals long since extinct. Here too she discovers the birds and the flowers, in elevated areas where spring blossoms are just beginning to blanket the sloping meadows in late July.

Offbeat Oregon isn't written for the traveler in a hurry. It's a handbook for the dawdler, the laggard, the undisciplined explorer who can be herded down a primrose-lined path by a butterfly, and never regret a minute of it!

MARJE BLOOD

ACKNOWLEDGMENTS

My sincere thanks to everyone who gave me what was always cheerful assistance; to Grace Gordon, who likes to explore back lanes, too; to Sue Riemer, who uncomplainingly swallowed Eastern Oregon dust with me; to Mary Ann Campbell, of the Medford *Mail Tribune,* who knows all the back roads of Jackson County; to Richard H. Engeman, Librarian and Archivist of the Southern Oregon Historical Society; to John Scharff of Burns, for allowing me to quote part of his story about Pete French; to John Hoffnagle of The Nature Conservancy and to Louise Morley, for introducing me to lovely Cascade Head; to Marje Blood, for her ever-authoritative advice; and most of all to my grown-up offspring, Jean Bell and Robert Bell, for their steady encouragement.

INTRODUCTION

Oregonians are accustomed to magnificence in their scenery. In almost any part of Oregon, white-capped peaks are either in view or not far from it. About 100 miles inland from the coast, the Cascades march south through Oregon in virtually a straight line. At 11,245 feet, Mount Hood is Oregon's highest peak, but Mount Jefferson, some forty miles to the south, comes within five feet of reaching the 11,000-foot level. Each of the Three Sisters tops 10,000 feet, and Mount McLoughlin, at the southern end of the state, rises 9495 feet above sea level.

The wide Columbia River forms Oregon's northern boundary; the Snake River, which plunges through North America's deepest canyon, defines most of its eastern border. The Siskiyou Mountains stand in the southwestern corner, where Oregon meets California, and the Pacific Ocean crashes against a shoreline that, counting all its wriggling ins and outs, measures 429 miles.

An hour's drive from Oregon's largest cities takes you to a seaside beach or a mountain pass. If Oregonians occasionally seem to take their environment for granted, the time they spend at the edge of the sea and along mountain trails belies the notion. They are used to it all, but they love it. They are also tremendously proud of Oregon's history — of its beginnings at the mouth of the Columbia and of its oldest towns in the Willamette Valley, that promised land for the pioneers who jounced across the continent by covered wagon — and they take nostalgic pride in whatever is reminiscent of an earlier day, from an aging lighthouse to a gold-rush ghost town.

The rugged individual is said to be nearly extinct, but if you go looking for one, start in Oregon. The pace here is a bit slower than average. It's hard to hurry an Oregonian. He — or she — likes a touch of leisure in the day. His — or her — preference is usually a back road rather than a freeway, quite possibly a bicycle instead of a car, and wilderness trails are full of those who are aware that the best way to know the country is to walk it.

All Oregonians have their favorite locales. In a book this size, space allows for just a handful of such places. But come along and poke around a few — whenever possible by the back way, the offbeat way, the never-in-a-hurry way. You are all welcome.

1
Along the Edge
of the Pacific

A black-hulled freighter against the sunset is a familiar scene at the Astoria docks.

For 350 miles U.S. 101 follows the Pacific from the Columbia River to California, passing beside crescent beaches, over high promontories, along golden hills of sand, and through pastoral meadows. By car, by bike, or on foot, when you take time to look, surprises are everywhere. Perhaps the shell of a frilled dogwinkle to hold in your hand, the spume of a spouting horn as waves crash into a rock defile, or the thin geyser of a spouting whale. Or, when the sea air has made you ravenous, a small cafe where the clam chowder, redolent of the sea, or an extra-special hamburger can suddenly satisfy the soul.

For most of the way, the highway runs near the ocean — sometimes high above it, more often close to beaches and coves where jumbles of driftwood mark the tides' furthest thrust, and for forty miles south of Florence along the tawny sand dunes that are Oregon's own Sahara. State parks and waysides for campers, picnickers, and beachcombers offer access to the beach, all of which is public domain in Oregon. Parts of the southern coastline are inaccessible simply because of their ruggedness. Occasionally, but rarely, it is necessary to cross private property to reach the ocean, but every beach the length of the coast is open to you to explore — for free.

Accommodations range from beach cottage to lodge and condominium, and eating places from deli to candle-lit dining room. Some favorite places begin at the mouth of the Columbia River.

ASTORIA:
Where It All Began

On a sunny day in May 1792, Robert Gray, out from Boston in his eighty-three-foot sloop, sailed blithely across the Columbia bar, and Oregon was all but born. For nearly three centuries explorers had passed the river either without seeing it, or, suspecting its presence, unable to enter its forbidding mouth.

Captain Gray took his ship right across it, sailing, as he wrote in his log, "east-north-east between the breakers, having some five to seven fathoms of water. When we were over the bar, we found this to be a large river of fresh water, up which we steered . . ."

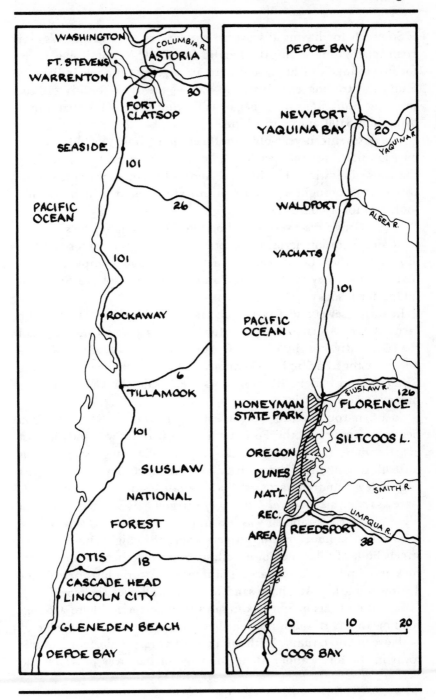

So much for having discovered the largest river in the Western Hemisphere to flow into the Pacific Ocean! The captain had come for furs to take to China, and here among the Chinook Indians he found the trading excellent. He named the river for his 212-ton ship, the *Columbia,* and began collecting otter skins that would bring him $100 apiece in China.

Gray's seventeen-year-old subofficer, John Boit, scribbled in his own journal that "the beach was lin'd with natives, who ran along the shore following the ship . . . Above 10 canoes came off," he wrote, "and brought a good lot of furs and salmon, which last they sold, two for a board nail."

It was Gray's discovery that boosted Thomas Jefferson's plan to send an expedition across the continent, and by the winter of 1805-06, Meriwether Lewis and William Clark had completed their incredible journey to the Pacific and had settled down a few miles inland for a soggy season.

In turn, Lewis and Clark's successful exploration inspired John Jacob Astor to further his plans for a trading post on the banks of the "Great River of the West." By April 1811, a small group of partners in Astor's Pacific Fur Company had arrived by sea on the little *Tonquin* and had built a log stockade beside the Columbia and named it Fort Astoria.

So when you explore Oregon, start in Astoria, where Oregon began. A replica of the Fort Astoria stockade now stands almost exactly where the original did at 15th and Exchange streets. It is difficult to visualize the dock that once extended beyond the river's edge a few hundred yards from the small bastion. As Charles H. Carey says in his *General History of Oregon,* "It was situated in a bight of the river, and so was less subject to boisterous waves."

Now traffic hums on busy streets where that bight used to be — streets built of fill, much of it ballast from ships that dumped their rock and sand to take on cargoes of lumber. Astoria historian Roger Tetlow remarks, "We have sand here from all over the world."

Go out on Clatsop Spit, six miles west of Astoria, where a paved road meanders through the marshes, with spurs out to the edge of both ocean and estuary. With sand and salt grass underfoot and salt spray in the air, wander along the edge of the river to watch the

Fishermen on Clatsop Spit try for bottom fish off the six-mile-long South Jetty at the mouth of the Columbia River.

great, black-hulled freighters pass close by. Some of those cargo ships are 400 feet long. Imagine what it must have been like to cross the bar's maelstrom of waters in a small sailing ship before the north and south jetties stretched their long, curving arms into the ocean. Built at the turn of the century, the south jetty reaches some six miles seaward, halting at least some of the ocean's fury; the north arm extends two-and-a-half miles.

When Lewis and Clark arrived at the Pacific in the winter of 1805 -06 and camped for a while on the Washington side of the Columbia, Clark remarked in his journal, "I can't say Pacific, as since I have seen it, it has been the reverse." It roared, he said, "like a repeated rolling thunder."

On a day of wind and tide you will find it thundering, too. Climb the high, wooden platform close beside the south jetty, and you may be showered with the spray from waves crashing against the jetty's enormous boulders. But on a day when the Pacific warrants its name, booted fishermen clamber over the rocks to try for bottom fish.

"What have you got?" one calls to another, who is swinging a pail. "Oh, just some starfish for the kids," the other replies. "Not fishing today."

Over on the Washington shore is the Cape Disappointment light — the oldest standing lighthouse on the West Coast — and high above Astoria, on Coxcomb Hill, rises the famous, 125-foot-high Astoria Column, its spiraling panels engraved with the area's dramatic history. It's fun to use binoculars to watch the cars zipping across the Astoria Bridge, which spans the Columbia for four-and-one-tenth miles from Oregon to the Washington shore. In 1966 the bridge replaced the ferries that used to take passengers across the wide river on leisurely miniature voyages. The world moves faster and faster!

A glimpse of life on the raw edge of the continent almost two centuries ago can be most enjoyable discovered at the Columbia River Maritime Museum (open 9:30 a.m. to 5:00 p.m. every day) at 17th Street and Maritime Drive. The museum's spacious new building, shaped like the dip and crest of an ocean wave, opened on May 11, 1982, exactly 190 years to the day when Yankee Captain Gray found the Columbia bar in a comparatively mild-mannered mood.

Look for the precisely fashioned plank-on-frame model of Gray's three-masted ship, the *Columbia Rediviva of Boston.* How did the crew ever manage all that complicated rigging? And how frail she looks to have slipped through the breakers running north-south across that meeting place of mighty river and often stormy sea that would come to be called the "graveyard of the Pacific."

Other models and beautifully painted pictures bring alive those seafaring days when wind-powered ships first plied the waters of the then untamed river. Here, in miniature, is the 290-ton *Tonquin,* which Astor sent out to establish his settlement beside the Columbia. Eight men were lost before the *Tonquin* made it across the bar in the spring of 1811, an omen perhaps of the tragic end she met the following year, when she was blown up during a violent battle with Indians off Vancouver Island.

How delicate His Majesty's two-masted armed tender, the *Chatham,* in which Captain George Vancouver's lieutenant, William R. Broughton, sailed up the Columbia not long after Gray's brief visit.

Astoria stretches beside the Columbia River, crossing it by a four-mile bridge. The city's history is on a hilltop monolith.

He surveyed the river meticulously, named a snowy peak Mount Hood and a site on the Washington coast Vancouver, and claimed it all for Britain.

Have a look, too, at the broken, copper-sheathed keel timber of H.M.S. *Raccoon,* a British sloop of war. The *Raccoon* came to the mouth of the Columbia during the War of 1812, ready and more than willing to blow Fort Astoria into the sea. The ship's captain, William Black, was quite disappointed to find the British flag already flying above the little fort — Astor's men, threatened with seizure, had sold out to Britain's North West Company. "Great God," Black is said to have exclaimed. "I could batter it down with a four-pounder in two hours!"

For five years then, the settlement was called Fort George; but in 1818, after each side in the war had given back what it had grabbed

The red-hulled Columbia, *which served for twenty-eight years as river lightship off the mouth of the Columbia River, has a permanent home on the Astoria waterfront.*

The huge 25,000-pound anchor from the battleship Indiana *sets the theme at the Columbia River Maritime Museum. A corner of the big shingled building is at right, the stern of the* Columbia *at left.*

from the other, the Stars and Stripes flew above the fort once more, and it was Astoria for keeps.

Plan to spend some time at the museum, for it is an exciting place. The gigantic, 25,000-pound anchor (from the U.S. battleship *Indiana*) in front of the museum sets the mood. The museum building had literally to wrap itself around the huge wheelhouse and bridge of the destroyer U.S.S. *Knapp.* The wheelhouse of a river steamer — the kind that steamed up and down the Columbia during the 1880s and 1890s — has been faithfully recreated. One of the most popular exhibits is the conning tower, with two periscopes, from the World War II submarine U.S.S. *Rasher.* Look into the periscopes to see what is happening out on the river and to get a close-up of the red-hulled Coast Guard lightship *Columbia,* docked beside the museum plaza. Your ticket to the museum also admits you to the lightship, Number 604, retired in 1979 after twenty-eight years of duty.

When retired, she was the last lightship serving on the West Coast, also the fourth and last to be called *Columbia River Lightship.* The first was stationed off the bar in 1892. Lightship 604 was built expressly for service at the mouth of the Columbia, that "graveyard" where some 200 ships have been lost. Since December 1980, she has had a permanent home beside the museum. Gaze up at the masts, where powerful lights used to guide sailors, and wander through the ship's living quarters to see where her sixteen-member crews slept, ate, and worked on their long, forty-two-day tours of duty.

Now an automated navigational buoy, forty-two feet high and forty feet in diameter, has taken the place of the *Columbia.* Though it may have a very efficient light, radio beacon, and fog signal, what romance is there in a huge mechanical gadget swaying in the waves? Whenever the Coast Guard cutter *Yocona* is in port, she also docks alongside the lightship, which gives you a near if limited glimpse of Coast Guard life on the river in the 1980s.

As befits a city grown from the first American settlement on the West Coast, Astoria treasures its heritage. Some fine old houses have been restored since the prodigal days when fisheries and salmon canneries brought wealth to the region. Built on the city's steep hills above the river, these homes were high enough to have escaped the devastating fire of 1922, which destroyed thirty-two business blocks. The Chamber of Commerce provides walking-tour maps that locate a number of them.

*Captain Flavel's wife kept the light going in the
cupola of their home when her husband was
piloting ships across the Columbia bar.*

Queen of the lot is the Flavel Mansion, built in 1883. Since 1953 it
has been the home of the Clatsop County Historical Society, which
has furnished it in all the opulence of the last century. Mannequins
in period costumes are arranged here and there in spacious rooms
with fourteen-foot ceilings, and Persian rugs cover the floors. The
six fireplaces are framed in exotic, hand-carved wood, each one set
with tiles imported from a different country. In enormous paintings
sailing ships slash through mountainous seas. Mementos in the
"Chinese Room" recall the 1890s, when 2000 Chinese lived in the
area, most of them working in the fish canneries for fifteen dollars a
month.

Captain George Flavel, river pilot, merchant, and art collector,
brought an architect and shipbuilders from San Francisco to build

The dining room of the Flavel mansion under its glittering chandelier looks out through the solarium onto luxurious gardens.

the mansion at Eighth and Duane streets. Had Queen Victoria herself seen it, surely she would have approved of its rococo gables, cornices, and porches, its high, narrow windows and tall chimneys. The captain was noted for his skill as a river pilot and once was awarded a gold medal for heroic action in rescuing survivors from the *General Warren,* the first steamboat lost crossing the bar. His wife, they say, used to keep the light going in the fourth-story cupola when he was bringing in a ship. An unfinished third floor apparently was planned as a ballroom, but Captain Flavel died just six years after moving into his elegant home. A picture of the captain and his wife — she was very pretty — hangs in the first floor hall.

Some four miles southwest of Astoria — follow the signs from U.S. 101 — an absorbing "living history" program is enacted from Memorial Day through Labor Day at Fort Clatsop National Memorial. National Park rangers in buckskin and coonskin caps relive routine activities that kept Lewis and Clark and their band of explorers busy during the wet winter of 1805-06 — so wet indeed that on only 12 days out of 106 did it fail to rain.

A log stockade has been built, based on drawings from the Lewis and Clark diaries. It is a copy of the one the explorers finished just in time for Christmas in December 1805. Today it represents a memorial to those men, precursors of the overland fur traders, of the pioneers, and of Oregon.

Here, within the enclosure, are small cabins, each with a crude fireplace. One is a replica of the cabin shared by the two leaders, who spent so much time recording everything they found, from salal berries to a beached whale. Another was for the Charbonneaus — Sacajawea, the expedition's guide; her husband, Toussaint, who acted as interpreter; and their small son, Baptiste. Other cabins provided sleeping quarters for eight men at a time.

Rangers carry out camp chores as they had to be done nearly two centuries ago. They tan elk and deer hides, make candles, shape musket balls of melted lead, and cure elk jerky. Jerky may have been the most palatable form of elk the explorers had, for Clark wrote in his journal that their meat was "pore Elk, so much spoiled that we eate it thro' mear necessity."

Gates to the memorial are open from 8:00 a.m. to 8:00 p.m. during the summer season and from 8:00 a.m. to 5:00 p.m. the rest of the year; summer activities continue from 9:00 a.m. to 5:30 p.m. daily.

Not exactly deluxe, but Lewis and Clark expedition members survived in cabins like this during the soggy winter of 1805 and 1806.

*From the "Penacle," Cascade Head climbs
gradually away from the ocean.*

CASCADE HEAD:
Trails to Grassy Uplands

Among the great promontories along the Oregon shore, Cascade
Head, in the Siuslaw National Forest, is one of the loveliest. About
six miles north of Lincoln City, it rises just beyond the mouth of the
Salmon River to the Pinnacle — often spelled "Penacle," as it appeared on the first geographic maps — some 500 feet straight up
from the breakers. The promontory then climbs away from the
ocean until it reaches its highest point at 1565 feet above sea level.

By a 1974 Act of Congress, the first Scenic-Research Area in the
United States was established here, thereby assuring that no new
development would disturb the rare ecology of the region. Within
this area, which is administered by the Hebo Ranger District office
of the Siuslaw National Forest, 280 acres of grassland belong to The
Nature Conservancy. The research area also includes a United Na-
tions Biosphere Reserve — one of twenty-eight in the United States —
and a Research Natural Area.

Three trails climb through spruce and hemlock forest to the
grassy highlands for exciting ocean views. The North Trail, which
climbs to the top of Cascade Head, is reached by an old gravel road,

Forest Service Road S1861, that turns west off U.S. 101 about nine miles north of Lincoln City. Follow the road for three miles, bearing left where it forks off to a viewpoint. The trailhead is about three-quarters of a mile past the fork. A large sign and interpretive map mark the entrance.

The trail winds through groves of red alder where the branches meet overhead. "It reminds me of a wedding procession under crossed swords," remarks one hiker.

The trail also snakes through a forest of Sitka spruce, with giant specimens that are five feet in diameter and probably 250 years old. Above the woods, slopes are free of trees and wild grasses grow tall. As you climb toward the ocean, its muffled roar grows louder, and the air takes on that biting freshness born of the salty westerlies. Views of the Pacific far below are grand.

The North and South trails meet on the Head, and a third one, toughest of all, leads to Hart's Cove, where Chitwood Creek Falls drops away for 200 feet or so down to the sea. The tiny, horseshoe-shaped cove is a delightful place of mosses, ferns, and wildflowers.

The "Penacle" itself — Cascade Head's farthest western thrust — is closed. It was fenced off originally by farmers to keep their cattle and sheep from falling over the cliffs; now the fence protects endangered plant species, such as the sea-bluff campion and the catchfly. The latter is said to grow on the coast only here and on Cape Lookout. Several species of plants on the Head are unique because the isolation of the promontory prevents their interbreeding with plants on other headlands or on lower elevations.

So hikers are urged to stay on the trails. Both The Nature Conservancy and the Forest Service warn that once the vegetation has been trampled and soil erosion has begun, many years will be needed to repair the damage.

Midsummer is the great time here when the purple foxgloves stand tall, reaching out from tangles of grass and yarrow, and clumps of daisies and Queen Anne's lace along the road banks. A doe may lope away as you interrupt her browsing, and if you're quite lucky, a coterie of guinea hens — strays that wander over the hillsides of the Cascade Ranch area — will run a waddling race with you down the road.

Stray guinea hens run races with visitors on Three Rocks Road, one of the routes to Cascade Head trails.

In one of those short country pieces that appear now and then in England's *Manchester Guardian,* Ralph Whitlock wrote about the things of summer in a July 1982 issue: "The way to enjoy a summer is to forget, as far as possible, the neat little parcels into which we package our time. Winter is long and summer is short; let us open the windows of all our senses to the present."

A good philosophy, that, as you climb the lush slopes of Cascade Head.

SITKA CENTER:
Where Art and Nature Meet

At the Sitka Center for Art and Ecology, which is located on the shoulder of Cascade Head, some exciting classes are open to all age groups every summer during June and July. Experts in the fields of art and ecology conduct outdoor workshops on such topics as plant identification, the plant communities of Cascade Head, the ecology of Sitka spruce, and the coastal forest canopy. A three-day class in bird observation includes leisurely walks on the Head to various habitats to identify birds and to learn about their behavior, migration, and origins.

Recent class offerings include calligraphy and wood block print-making, Amish quilt design, Siletz Indian basketry, ceramic tile making, relief woodcarving, painting with water colors, even astronomy. The program focuses on the relationship between art and nature, and whenever possible workshops are held out-of-doors. Some classes are planned for children and for novices; others are for advanced artists. They range in length from a day to a week, but most run two to three days, often over weekends. Class fees vary, and it is wise to register early because the vacation-time program has become very popular.

For more information, write to the Neskowin Coast Foundation, P.O. Box 65, Otis, Oregon 97368.

THE OTIS CAFE:
The Hamburgers Aren't Squashed

Appetites usually go berserk when you're traveling, and it's a comfort to know where your next meal is coming from. So arrange to have one come from the little cafe at Otis Junction. You'll be glad you did.

The junction is located on State Highway 18, three miles east of Lincoln City, and is well worth the short detour from U.S. 101 if you are traveling along the coast. Watch closely, because there is only a tiny highway sign and the small post office next door to the cafe to let you know that you are in Otis.

You also could make the mistake of passing the cafe right by — a pity — for it makes no claim to being special. Its big sign simply says "Cafe," but the building is painted an old-fashioned barn red, with bright flowers and herbs in a box by the door.

The Cafe beside the highway at Otis Junction surprises drop-in customers with epicurean fare.

Except for quiche and occasionally moussaka, even the menu looks standard enough — hamburgers, cheeseburgers, and the like — but there's a difference! Virginia Morgan, owner and cook, has a knack for turning everyday food into epicurean fare. Ask why the hamburgers are so exceptional, and she probably will tell you that the meat is always fresh, that she seasons and forms the patties herself, and that she doesn't squash them down on the grill. Indeed she believes that most people don't treat meat like meat; they treat it like sawdust.

And the bread! Kneading a great batch of dough at the back of the shop, the attractive chef says the bread is simply "our standard cafe whole-wheat . . . I use just enough oatmeal to hold it together." The mixture produces bread as bread should be: grain rich but light, and always fresh. She bakes sixty pounds a week.

The cinnamon rolls, chocolate-chip cookies, pies, and walnut oatmeal cake — all from scratch — measure up to the same high standard, and so do the beef stew served with salad and that wonderful bread, the fish chowder made with tender white fish, the hearty navy-bean soup, and the fluffy omelettes properly made with two eggs to the omelette and a choice of ham, bacon, cream cheese, tomatoes, onions, or a lot of other things, including sauteed seasonal vegetables.

Fresh flowers on windowsills, softly played classical music, magazines such as the *New Yorker* on one rack, and books for youngsters on another, make the Otis Cafe a pleasant place in which to linger. It is open from 7:00 a.m. to 3:00 p.m. Monday through Wednesday; 7:00 a.m. to 9:00 p.m. Thursday through Saturday; and 8:00 a.m. to 9:00 p.m. Sunday.

THE MARKETPLACE: Hot Pots and Scribbles

It is a pleasure to wander through the inviting shops of the Marketplace at Gleneden Beach. On the west side of U.S. 101, across from Salishan Lodge, the complex has a couple of dozen shops and a pleasant restaurant with tables overlooking Siletz Bay.

Benches encourage leisure along walkways bright with flowers, and the shop names alone are entertaining. Against the Wall specializes, naturally, in paintings, prints, and posters, and Hot Pots offers clay casseroles and candy molds, copper pots and woks, dainty French egg cups and that ultimate luxury in the kitchen, marble rolling pins! The picnic baskets are reminiscent of the hampers kept on hand for royal outings at London's Fortnum and Mason.

Free-standing shelves at the Allegory Book Shop let you see the entire cover of a book at first glance, not just its narrow spine. Notepapers at Scribbles come in soft-hued designs, and Between Friends has a great collection of baskets, cotton rugs from India, and lovely pastel candles.

These are only a few of the many shops, of course, and after you've seen everything, you may want to sit at one of the small tables at the Coast Roast Coffee Company, which roasts beans in a huge roaster on the premises. When you are sampling a brew or having a cuppa with crumpets and honey, try the special apple muffins — or the Viennese butter cake.

Ground flavorings for coffee-making at home — including almond, cinnamon, chocolate-mint, and chocolate-cognac — are sold here by the ounce; two-and-a-half ounces to the pound is the suggested proportion.

Charter fishing boats hurry home through Depoe Bay's narrow, rock-squeezed channel.

DEPOE BAY: A Sea-Salty Town

"Four swells and seven white caps ago, our Skipper brought forth onto this ocean the *Tradewinds Kingfisher,* conceived in seaworthiness and dedicated to the proposition that — everybody should have a good time on it."

So writes Skipper Stan Allyn in the log he keeps for passengers on his short ocean cruises out of Depoe Bay. And everybody does have a good time.

Novices go down to the sea in cruise boats, fishermen in charter boats from Depoe Bay's tiny harbor — the "smallest navigable harbor in the world." The great thing for a fisherman chugging out of the harbor is that once he crosses the narrow channel under the bridge, he is at sea. In minutes he may have some kind of bottom fish on the end of his line — red snapper, sea bass, ling cod, or any number of others, even halibut. In season, of course, salmon is the prize. The charters take anglers out year-round, weather permitting, and that is generally a good 75 percent of the time.

Cruise trips are for landlubbers and whale watchers. About a dozen are going out today on the *Kingfisher,* though she can accommodate twenty-nine.

"I've been out before, but *she* is scared to death," announces a young man, nodding toward the girl he has brought along.

The boat moves smartly under the highway bridge and heads straight for Japan. The mid-May sun is warm, but the wind is brisk, and this does not happen to be one of those lazy, three-to-six-foot-wave days. Swells are rolling in at more like eight and ten feet, and you need to hang on to something. Captain Allyn says that anybody who wishes may move to the small upper deck. Everybody does, and up there you hang on with both hands.

The *Kingfisher,* which looked so big at dockside, seems to have shrunk. But she rides the waves with a graceful ease, dipping low into the deep troughs, then rising with a splash atop the next watery hill.

"Wonder how many have gone over the rail," muses the man who has "been out before." His companion, who has yet to utter a word, shivers. Down to the sea in ships is not for everybody, but it is for most of these laughing passengers. The boat passes a swaying ocean buoy, its bell gonging lugubriously, and then another, which repeats and repeats its single high note. Is the sound really so melancholy, or has literary tradition created that expectation? Where is that tone on the scale? It can't be far off a tuning fork's A. Is it B flat? But soon the note is lost in the sounds of splashing water, the boat's creaking ligaments and the high-pitched squeals of these sailors-for-a-day. Curiously, Mr. Nonchalance has gone slightly gray about the jowls; he lurches his way to the stairs and goes below, his silent partner in tow.

The captain is saying, "You are now beyond the three-mile limit of the United States — three miles from shore but only 200 feet from land." As she turns, the sturdy craft takes a couple of swells that roll her sideways. Then she eases into the waves, the wind at her back, and everyone goes back to a cushioned seat on the lower deck to

Kingfisher *Captain Stan Allyn has a pipe on the Channel House deck after skippering a landlubber cruise.*

hear the skipper relate some salty facts as he steers the *Kingfisher* for that narrow, rock-squeezed gorge and home.

The captain says that the Pacific is the world's largest ocean, covering 64 million square miles, and that in 1934 in mid-Pacific the *U.S.S. Ramapo* recorded the world's highest wave, 112 feet high. These world-famous fishing waters off the Oregon coast, he says, contain 287 varieties of fishes.

Stan Allyn, who founded Trade Winds Trollers in 1938, looks the part of a proper skipper: bronzed, confident, a pipe between his teeth.

"I never smoke anything else," he says, giving a loving look at the pipe in his hand. "I couldn't smoke a cigarette, but my pipe's like an old friend."

The *Kingfisher* has sailed smoothly into port, and now those forty minutes at sea seem hardly to have lasted ten. Except for gray-around-the-jowls, who is first on the dock, the cruise passengers clamber ashore reluctantly and climb the long stairway from harbor to highway. Fishermen from other boats have had their catches cleaned and cut on the docks, and they trudge slowly up the stairs, their heavy loot in plastic bags over their shoulders.

No whales spotted today on the sightseeing cruise. By early May most of the gray whales have already passed this part of the coast on the incredible 6000-mile journey to the Bering Sea from lagoons in Baja California, where they have wintered. Earlier, in March and April, these mini-voyages three miles from shore afford some exciting views, for gray whales swim fairly close to shore on their migrations. Traveling in small pods at an average speed of four knots an hour, fifteen or so may pass by within an hour. The grays are baleen whales, which strain their food through long screens of whalebone hanging from their upper palates. A mottled gray, these whales are usually covered with barnacles, particularly around their heads. They feed in icy Arctic waters from June through October, then begin once more the long trip back to the warm lagoons. There they will breed, and the females will bear the calves they have carried for a year. Fortunately the grays, once killed by the hundreds, are now protected by international law.

There is something most appealing about this sea-salty little town and its cozy harbor. It could hardly be closer to the ocean — its main

*At sea-salty little Depoe Bay, this is a typical
summer's day.*

A harbor seal in the Depoe Bay Aquarium offers eye-to-eye encounters with visitors.

street is the highway, bordered by the sea wall. When winter winds and tides are high, waves sometimes splash over into the street. The long bridge at the south end of town crosses the precarious channel separating tiny harbor from vast sea, and people hang over the railings to watch boats dance in and out. Down there below, a man is swabbing the deck of his fishing boat, crews are cutting fish on the dock, and a proud angler is holding up a ling cod to have his picture taken for posterity.

This compact community crowds a remarkable lot of shops and eating places into its short stretch of business blocks opposite the sea wall and up the hill to both the north and south. The small saltwater aquarium, opened in 1927, can still be visited every day but Christmas. It has one large seal tank and a few small tanks. The octopuses, so incredibly ugly, are fascinating. One seems to like to sulk in a corner, another to plaster his eight arms against the glass. But the seals are the fun here. At the entrance, buy some herring chips to feed them, and they will give you a briny show. Below the low glass partition around their tank, these sea clowns stand on their tails, with just their heads out of the water; their large, unblinking eyes stare you into going out to get another pack of herring. It's a wonderful place for youngsters.

Depoe Bay restaurants open at dawn for the avid angler. The Chowder Bowl claims their is the "best" clam chowder around, and, indeed, it is smooth, just thick enough, creamy, and the clams cut-with-a-spoon tender.

A couple of kibitz-ers supervise the cutting up of the catch from a charter boat.

"How is it your clams are never tough?" the chef is asked.

"They're always fresh," he replies, "and I don't boil them too long."

"How about another bowl?"

Clam fritters are the specialty up the hill at the North Point Cafe. A small cafe ringed with windows, the North Point is a cozy place for whale watching. The view is of a crescent cove at the rocky tip of which fierce rip tides gather.

"Gray whales come in so close sometimes that you can clearly see the barnacles on them," says Joyce Stanek, who, with her husband, Rex, owns the restaurant. "Killer whales come in sometimes — they are beautiful — but mostly the grays. Every now and then one comes in and plays around as though it just wanted to relax for a while."

One of the most exciting things to watch in Depoe Bay is a Coast Guard training session.

"We usually practice on Fridays," says Chief Wayne Bauer, the man in charge of the attractive, small station on the east side of the harbor. So look for them from the esplanade along the sea wall. They usually practice just off the spouting horn, which in high tide sends up geysers of spume.

It is a bit startling to see a nineteen-ton, forty-four-foot boat cap-size and then right itself. Does it always work?

The chief laughs. "I've never had one that wouldn't come around yet," he says. And Bauer should know, for he has served with the Coast Guard from Port Isabel, Texas, near the Mexican border, to Depoe Bay, with Brookings, Gold Beach, and Winchester stations in between. And he likes Depoe Bay best, perhaps because its harbor entrance is "one of the most treacherous on the coast. We always have a boat outside the channel in rough water," he says.

You also may see the station's ten-ton thirty-six-footer rolling over in the waves out there. Built in 1951, and the only one its size left in the Coast Guard, it is Bauer's favorite. "It has a lower profile," he says, "and doesn't wobble around so much." But he may come to prefer the thirty-footers that were introduced for Coast Guard use in 1983.

Seashore-oriented souvenirs made from shells — the aquarium has an excellent collection — to Greek fishermen's hats crowd the shelves of stores along the highway. Saltwater taffy seems to be everywhere — it is made in the window of one shop every day.

Depoe Bay artist Richard Hazelton has an attractive gallery in a wing of his home up the hill to the north. His water colors have a special quality that captures the flavor of the Oregon littoral, the cool mists of a morning by the sea, or the warmth of a lazy afternoon on a tawny beach. The occasional tiny figures in Hazelton's paintings have a remarkable mobility.

"I spend a lot of time on the beach in summer sketching people," he says. "I watch what they do and how they move. Then in winter I paint."

Be sure to visit Jean Quinn's Channel Book Shop at the south end of the bridge on the ocean side. There's nothing quite like it. The store is a block long — granted, a short one, but a block just the same. It is a labyrinth of books: new, used, hardback, and paperback. Ask the owner, whose black cat lies contentedly atop a stack of books at her desk, if she knows how many volumes she has. She will probably tell you, "I haven't counted them lately."

Among the book categories listed above each open doorway into five large rooms is the message "Keep going. Welcome." In room three, romances are listed so: "Clean, Harlequin, Cartland, Doctor's." The fourth room holds "Mysteries, Westerns, Northwesterns,

Best Romance, and Adventure." Keep going! Room five has what appears to be several tons of *National Geographic*s. Taped up here and there, wherever there's a vacant spot, are hilarious cartoons from the *New Yorker*. They make the wandering even more fun.

A customer, dizzied perhaps by the sheer quantity of books, asks the owner for an Amanda Cross whodunit. The response comes quickly: "Did you get into the fifth room on the west side of the free-standing cabinet?"

The Channel Book Shop is a Depoe Bay tradition, open every day except Thanksgiving and Christmas. Good browsing.

The Channel House is a delightful surprise, one of the most charming places on the Oregon coast in which to stay. The modest-looking, gray-shingled inn is perched on a low bluff above the ocean at the south end of the bridge, where the fifty-foot-wide channel cuts through the rocky shore to the harbor. Once an apartment house, the building had stood empty and neglected for years until it stirred the imagination of Paul Schwabe, a Portland realtor. Schwabe bought the place, tore it apart, and transformed it into a seaside inn, with all the charm and comfort that the name implies.

Its seven rooms are simple and civilized, with cozy comforters on the beds, good reading lights, and a striking piece of fabric on the wall of each room accenting its decor. Three rooms are very small, but each has its piece of ocean in view; two are medium in size, and two are commodious suites with their own oceanfront decks, a hot tub on one of them. Each suite has a fireplace in both the living room and bedroom and a dishwasher in the kitchen. Binoculars are provided for whale watching in the laziest possible fashion.

Breakfast is included for guests staying in the small rooms, and it is no continental soupçon of juice and a bun. Instead, juice comes by the whopping glassful, along with a generous plate of fruits in season plus sweet rolls or coffeecake. Have breakfast in bed or at the cozy oyster bar downstairs.

In the brick-floored dining room, you sit at sturdy tables made of hatch covers and look straight out to sea. You could be on ship-board. Ships' instruments of shining brass encourage the fantasy, but the pièce de résistance here is the oyster bar, behind which stands a tremendous cooler, a relic of the 1880s, that was discovered in a midwestern farmer's grocery store. Yaquina Bay oysters served on the half shell make a pleasant start for dinner, or try the oyster cocktail or stew, the oysters Rockefeller or oysters piquante.

Every year Depoe Bay stages two special events that attract great crowds. At the Indian Salmon Bake, held on the second Saturday in September, fresh salmon is cooked over beach fires, Indian-style, on the wide sands of Fogarty Creek State Park, two miles north of town.

The Fleet of Flowers is a quieter occasion. This beautiful ceremony has been conducted at Depoe Bay every Memorial Day since 1946. It began in memory of two local fishermen who had braved a frightful storm to help another try to bring his craft home. The two men lost their lives in the effort, while the beleaguered fisherman they had hoped to rescue managed to ride out the storm by tying his boat to a buoy. Now the ceremony commemorates all those who have lost their lives at sea. The impressive rites have become known in distant ports, and every year flowers come from all over the world to be cast upon the ocean.

The flowers are blessed by local clergy, the flag is lowered to half-mast, and taps is played by a bugler. Accompanied by a gun salute from the Oregon National Guard, vessels laden with flowers move slowly out of the harbor into the Pacific. One mile offshore the boats circle a Coast Guard cutter, and as jet fighters dip their wings, wreaths and masses of blooms are dropped onto the sea. It is a moving tribute, and often as many as 20,000 people come to Depoe Bay to witness it.

NEWPORT:
A Schooner and a Ghost

Oregonians know Newport by heart. They dig clams on Yaquina Bay State Park's wide sweep of sand. They take the kids to the Marine Science Center to meet the octopus and learn something about the Pacific. They go down to the crowded waterfront to stand in long queues in front of Mo's Annex for oyster stew, chowder, or pea-nut-butter cream pie, served family-style under a ceiling of fish nets.

They also watch as fishermen from charter boats carry their salmon to Jack's for canning, or lift their heavy plastic bags full of fish into the trunk of a car. They stand over a brick well of boiling water to see red crabs ladled out. And what they are really doing, all this time, is soaking up the atmosphere of a world that revolves around one thing — fishing.

Two attractions in Newport are quite special: the schooner *Sara,* tied up at Neptune's Wharf on the waterfront, and the old Yaquina Bay Lighthouse atop the hill in Yaquina Bay State Park.

Although she goes to sea occasionally, most of the time now the *Sara* lies quietly in harbor, her 4800 square feet of sail furled against the heavy gaff rails. But the two-masted ship has a long seafaring history since she was launched in Denmark in 1900. Newport owners Robert and Elaine Baker bought the ship in Germany. For a nomi-nal fee First Mate Paul Elliott will show you around.

The Danish-built schooner, Sara, *is open to visitors on the old-town waterfront in Newport.*

The *Sara* is full of rare antiques, including hand-carved chests and tables, some dating back to Spanish artisans of the seventeenth century. The ship is built of handsome woods, with four-inch oak planks on the outside and decks of Norwegian fir. One-hundred-one feet overall, the *Sara* has been transformed into a yacht. Captain, cabin boy, and galley used to be crowded into one small room behind a watertight wall, where the captain gave his orders by a system of bells.

"It was demeaning in the old days," Elliott explains, "for the captain to speak to his crew members. So he sent up orders by bells."

Where cargo used to be carried, now fourteen people can sleep in comfortable quarters. But squeeze into the fo'c's'le to imagine what it was like when the schooner was a working ship. There, on a beam, the words meaning "crew's quarters for two" are carved in Danish. For two? "Roughest ride in the boat up here, too," says the first mate.

When there's a storm raging overhead on a winter's night, unleashing a cacophony of creaks in the sixty-nine-foot-high main mast and the sixty-three-foot foremast, it starts the first mate writing poetry.

One poem begins, "When the wind blows through the riggin'/ The *Sara* seems to say/ I need brave an ocean wave/ I'm a prisoner on the bay."

The call of the sea, certainly, but the sailor-poet also was protesting the Jones Act, which forbids ships of foreign registry to engage in commerce in United States waters.

When you have wandered her decks, you, too, may wish that, "hull down for adventure," you might take to the sea below the *Sara*'s unfurled sails.

If you've first read the ghost story *The Haunted Light,* it's twice the fun, but even if you haven't, the old Yaquina Bay Lighthouse is an intriguing place to visit. The story, written by Joaquin Miller's sister, Lischen Miller, is a brief but exciting bit of fiction that was published in the *Pacific Monthly* in 1899. For a modest fee it is available in a paperback booklet at the Lincoln County Historical Museum, 545 S.W. 9th Street.

The bridge arches high above the bay at Newport. This view is from a Yaquina Bay State Park hillside.

In this tale, a beautiful young girl is left in Newport by her sea-faring father. She disappears in the lighthouse, leaving behind only a handkerchief and bloodstains on the stairs. When you climb those narrow, steep, and winding stairs to the "watchroom," where the keeper watched his light, perhaps you will wonder about that drop to the sea from . . . but there's no use spoiling the story!

One of the oldest buildings in Newport, the Yaquina Bay Lighthouse was built in 1871 as a harbor entrance light. The lantern, which probably burned whale oil, was installed in November of that year, but its beams were not visible to ships sailing south because of Yaquina Head. So in 1873 a new lighthouse was built on Yaquina Head, though only because somebody got mixed up and delivered building materials there instead of to Otter Crest, where the light was meant to be. The older light at the top of the bluff in what is now well-manicured Yaquina Bay State Park went out for good on October 1, 1874.

The old lighthouse must have been a busy place, however, during its three years of service, for lightkeeper Charles H. Pierce, who had been a captain in the Union Army, lived there with his wife and ten children. When the light was extinguished, he was transferred to the lighthouse at Cape Blanco.

Intermittently, life-saving crews, U.S. Army engineers, and the park caretaker used the house as headquarters. It was said to be chilly. It also stood empty as winter's storms widened its cracks, and for a while it looked as though it would be torn down. But it was a landmark, and Newport citizens, led by the county historical society, won a campaign to save it. Now nicely restored, it is furnished in the fashion of the 1870s, with a fireplace, four-poster bed, commode, and oak sea chest in the master bedroom, and a powder horn at the ready on the keeper's big desk downstairs.

Many pictures on the walls show how bleak that windswept cliff was when the lighthouse was built — not a tree around, where now the thick foliage of coastal pines almost surrounds the house.

Although not shown in his picture, lightkeeper Pierce, a Scotsman, is said to have worn a cap with ribbons down over his curls. His wife is pictured in a frilly cap tied under her chin, but she looks of sterner stuff than her Scottish husband. But then, between the years of 1851 and 1872, she produced those ten children. She may well have found life on the stern side.

The old Yaquina Bay Lighthouse is spruced up and cheery now, but some insist it harbors a ghost.

There used to be a zany song that asked, "Who takes care of the lighthouse keeper's daughter while the lighthouse keeper's busy keeping house?" With nine siblings, perhaps no problem?

Instructions to lighthouse keepers in 1871 directed that "lights are to be kept burning brightly, free from smoke . . . each entire night from sunset to sunrise," and that "during thick and stormy weather those keepers who have no assistants must . . . watch the light during the entire night."

Don't be surprised should you meet a Newport old-timer who insists, "Don't tell me there's no ghost up there. I've heard her nights when she's moaning. It's no place to be after dark."

A hostess at the historical museum understands this, for she used to work at the lighthouse on weekends. "When the fog swirled all around," she says, "and the rain beat against the windows, and the wind made all kinds of weird sounds, it was eerie. I used to sit by the door!"

Ghost or no ghost, fog or no fog, the lighthouse is a cheery place now; it is open afternoons over the Memorial Day weekend; again from 1 July through Labor Day; and by appointment for groups all year. Phone South Beach State Park, (503) 867-7451. The historical society museum — both Burrows House (circa 1895), which is the main headquarters, and the nearby log cabin — are open from 10:00 a.m. to 5:00 p.m. from June to October; 11:00 a.m. to 4:00 p.m. in winter months. Closed Mondays.

FLORENCE:
On a Spring Day

In early spring there always comes a day when everybody inland is getting impatient with the weather.

"Isn't it ever going to stop raining?" someone asks in Portland, or Salem, or Eugene. But the sun is shining on the coast, and somehow everybody knows. Suddenly the roads west are crowded.

Maybe it's a Sunday in mid-February.

"First good weekend we've had," someone in Eugene says, and

From Mo's windows on the Florence waterfront, old pilings and a beached boat have a melancholy appeal.

when you get to the beach beyond Florence, everybody is saying the same thing. The beach is a friendly place anytime, but on that first mild, almost-spring Sunday, everyone is smiling.

"Almost like summer," they say to one another.

At the south jetty a fisherman carrying a plastic pail is cautiously picking his way over the slippery boulders.

"Any luck?" asks a man watching him.

"Not much," answers the fisherman, sloshing half a dozen fish around in his pail. "Some bass, and these," he says, stopping to hold up a couple of samples.

"What's that one?"

"Be darned if I know. Never saw one like it before," and the angler shakes his head.

Back in Old Town people are window-shopping along Bay Street, or stopping in at Mo's for a chowder, and on the dock over the Siuslaw River, some scuba divers are getting a lot of attention. At the end of the dock in their shiny black skins, they are fastening helmets and goggles, but one is all business. He is already wading out into the water with a sack made of netting; the label on the sack reads "Onions."

"What's he going after?" a woman inquires, and a boy on the dock looks up.

"Crabs," he says, but his glance spells how-could-anybody-be-so-ignorant?

Then, a bit enviously, the boy asks a diver splashing about at the end of the pier, "Is it cold?"

"Not really," the man replies, water dripping off his beard. "Actually, it's great."

One of the spectators, seeing his chance to get into the conversation, offers, "The Japanese Current keeps it warm."

The divers pay him no mind, but another spectator chimes in with, "Sure, that's why it's such a nice day, while they're freezing in Maine."

Well, this is no day for arguing, but meteorologist Walter Rue, in his book *Weather of the Pacific Coast,* says the Japanese Current notion is a "myth."

"The truth is," he writes, that by the time it gets here, "the current is just a ribbon of slightly warm water in a cold ocean."

On the other side of the Pacific, the Japanese Current does indeed have a warming effect on the climate, Rue explains, but by the time it has "circled around toward the United States, it is a feeble force." It's the prevailing westerlies crossing great expanses of ocean, Rue says, that bring water vapors and temperatures like those of the sea to warm our shores.

All right, Mr. Rue, whatever you say. All we know is that today this is a warm and wonderful world. Children and dogs get their feet wet, cameras click, and the diver with his onion net has disappeared out there.

"Seals!" a man on the dock points out. "See," he says to the boy, who is still watching, and, sure enough, two dark heads have appeared on the surface.

"Out there around that piling there's a rock island you can't see. Seals hang around there."

Just then the diver surfaces out by the piling for just long enough to grin and wave. His friend on the pier waves back. "Guess he's doing all right."

"Those are the guys who get 'em," sighs another man who is watching it all. "I was out here at three o'clock this morning. At five o'clock I had only two crabs, so I went back to bed. But that way out there's not for me. Don't think I'd like it under all that water, and those seals around."

The man who knows these waters looks up with a laugh. "Oh, you ought to try it. It's another world down there. Like nothing else."

It will get cold on the way back to the valley. Only the reddening willow canes along the road hint of spring, while up ahead snow streaks the crest of the foothills. In Eugene it is not quite raining, only that light drizzle most Oregonians, more with affection than annoyance, call Oregon mist. But it was a beautiful day at the coast, the kind that promises a summer full of grand days ahead.

OREGON'S OWN SAHARA: A World of Rolling Sand

It's not every state that has its own Sahara, but Oregon does. Tall, rolling sand dunes, sometimes nearly 500 feet high, border the Pacific from Florence to Coos Bay, a distance of forty-one miles. At their widest, the dunes roll inland for about one-and-a-half miles, and 14,000 acres of these tawny hills are open sand. Since 1972 Oregon's oceanfront desert has been protected in the Oregon Dunes National Recreation Area, 32,000 acres in all, with headquarters in Reedsport.

The dunes rise in small mountains of sand, their architecture similar to the sea's own design. They billow up into smooth, rounded ridges, a golden spume blowing from their crests, then fall into deep-dipping gullies. It is a strangely beautiful world, changing as the light changes — almost white under a brilliant sun, soft gold of an afternoon, with shadows moving across the sand as the clouds move. The landscape is unique along the Pacific littoral. Why are they found only here along a shore made up chiefly of rugged bluffs and rocky indentations?

When the Coast Range was building, geologists explain, a wide shelf of pumice and ash not covered with lava pushed out across the ocean floor. Streams washed the sand into the ocean, tides washed it

*It's a world of sand and sky and sea on this section of
Oregon's coastal dunes south of Florence.*

ashore again, and westerly winds picked it up and blew it inland. This same game between stream, tide, and wind goes on and on inexorably.

Characteristically, the sand builds a foredune beside the beach, behind which a flat, marshy area called the deflation plain develops. Beyond this the dunes build inland as winds drop sand from the beach. When a slope reaches a 33-degree grade, sands flow down the side like water.

Geologists say that the Oregon dunes reached their peak of development about 6000 years ago. Now they continue to push inland from three to nine or ten feet a year. When they come too near to roads or riverbanks, typical forest vegetation is planted to stop them.

Early in the 1900s tough grass, used for the same purpose successfully in Europe, was planted on the foredunes. The grass, however, has spread so much, due to its remarkable root system, that now it is cutting off sand from the dunes, and "the dunes are dying," they say.

John Goold, National Recreation Area Resource Assistant, says that the policy has been to "let nature take its course," but both NRA and Oregon Fish and Wildlife researchers are working on the problem. Can they control the grass, they want to find out, or will they have to breach the foredunes that are now open only where streams flow out to the sea?

Visitors are encouraged to explore the dunes in their own way. Skillful drivers take squealing passengers up and over and down through the thick sands in hefty dune buggies, and off-the-road vehicles — most popular of all, the three-wheelers — tackle the slopes. Perhaps the most rewarding way is to trudge through the sand on foot.

"Where are the camels?" asks one hiker, laughing as he gazes over what appears to be an endless world of sand and sky.

It's an excellent idea to pick up maps and brochures from the Reedsport headquarters before you journey onto the sand. Maps show special trails, short routes to open sand from campgrounds such as Honeyman State Park on the edge of the recreation area, and other trails, including the mile-long hike from Siltcoos Beach Road across forest, dunes, and plain to the ocean. Fisherman's Trail from Waxmyrtle Campground traces the Siltcoos River on the way to the beach. Part of the recreation area is private property, so maps also help you avoid trespassing. And they indicate where off-the-road vehicles are allowed so that you won't head for dunes or beach only to find a sign telling you that you don't belong there.

Bordering the recreation area on the east is a series of freshwater lakes, formed when sand choked off waterway exits to the sea. Ten major lakes are popular with fishermen, boaters, and water skiers. Their waters are home to bass and blue gills, trout and crappies.

Obviously there's no dearth of things to do here, but often tourists on the Coast Highway drive right past the dunes without being aware of them, for strips of forest west of the road hide the sands.

"Do you know what question we get asked more than any other?" Goold asks. "It's 'Where are the dunes?'"

To answer it for everybody, an overlook was opened in August 1982; now travelers can get a fine view of dunes, deflation plain, and ocean from four levels of railing-enclosed platforms connected by wooden walkways. About halfway between Florence and Reedsport, the overlook also is the point at which the dunes come closest to the Coast Highway. An access road leads to a parking strip, and a trail leads down to the sand. Cozy sites along the trail provide picnic tables in the shade of fir and coastal pine, with views through the trees and across the sand to the ocean. It is only two-tenths of a mile to the dunes and a mile across sand and marsh to the beach. Once you've had a look, you're likely to want to get better acquainted with Oregon's Sahara.

A twenty-minute movie and slides are shown upon request at the NRA center in Reedsport. For information about campgrounds, fishing, trails, horseback-riding areas, the best ORV beaches, and dune locales, stop by or write to the Oregon Dunes National Recreation Area, 855 Highway Avenue, Reedsport, Oregon 97467.

2
Willamette Valley Glimpses

Coburg Inn, housed in this beautiful nineteenth-century former home, brings a little posh to a drowsy village.

Captain George Vancouver's lieutenant, William R. Broughton, found the Willamette River as he sailed up the Columbia in the autumn of 1792, but Lewis and Clark missed it both coming and going. Camped near the Sandy River on their homeward trip, they learned from Indians of a large stream that emptied into the Columbia, and Clark went back to see it. He went about ten miles up this river the Indians called *Multnomah,* historians believe, and he was so much impressed with its size that he thought it might originate in California.

By the late 1820s two French-Canadians, Etienne Lucier and Joseph Gervais, who had come with the Astor expedition and stayed on, were farming in the Willamette Valley. In

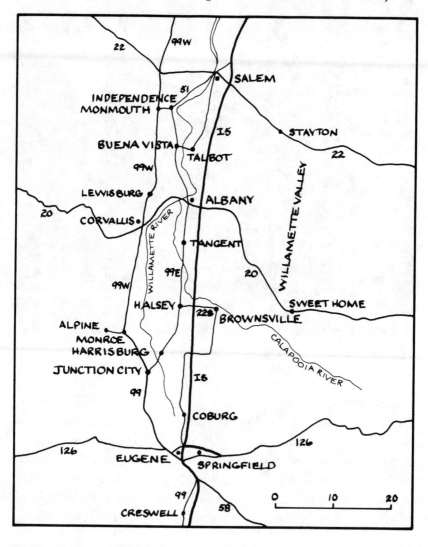

1834, the Reverend Jason Lee came to Oregon country to teach the "heathen" Indian, and he traveled up the Willamette Valley almost to what is now Salem. He had seeds given to him by Dr. John McLoughlin, Hudson's Bay factor at Fort Vancouver, and he, too, started a small farm.

By the 1840s the western migration was in full swing, and the 180-mile-long Willamette Valley, with its broad river, rich soil, and abundant timber, was their mecca. As towns grew up along its banks, the river became the pioneers' water road, and by the 1850s steamboats were puffing up and down it. Railroads soon changed the immigrants' way of life, however, and many of the river towns simply disappeared, while others became Oregon's chief cities.

The broad valley, sixty miles at its widest, is for discovering when you travel its country roads. Highways 99E and 99W, both a relief from the frenzied freeway, provide a sampling of quiet old towns, but the still more leisurely byways — those unnumbered black lines on road maps — seem so private they make you feel they belong to you. They open up a countryside sometimes as unfamiliar as that of another state.

A LAZY DAY:
On the Way to Salem

Interstate 5 runs straight north from Eugene to Salem over sixty-eight rather tiresome miles. Highway 99E goes the same way through such nice old towns as Junction City, Harrisburg, and Halsey and connects with the freeway at Albany. West of the Willamette River, 99W goes through Corvallis to the lovely old college town of Monmouth, with Independence right next door. The first settlers along the river at Independence came in 1845, and others followed at Monmouth eight years later, making these two of Ore-

This ancient car chugs through Coburg as old car buffs come to town; Dotson's Antiques across the street is one of their favorite destinations.

gon's oldest towns. The "little black roads" take you through hamlets along the way, pass occasional historical markers, and offer a taste of Cascade foothills, and one crosses the Willamette by a small and long-used ferry. So with map in hand, experiment a little, combining those black and red map routes for a lazy day on the way from Eugene to the state capital.

Take Coburg Road out of Eugene for the eight miles to that love of a town, named, according to Lewis A. McArthur in his *Oregon Geographic Names,* for a stallion the village smithy both admired and shod. Coburg is a hamlet for wandering. Drive around and discover its whopping old farmhouses and long-established gardens. The town has at least four antique shops — Dotson's is one of the most interesting — and just two places in which to eat, both on the main street and each a complete contrast to the other.

The Coburg Inn is located in a beautiful old home dating from the 1880s. The house has been expanded and refurbished and offers a touch of elegance. The Coburg Cafe, unimpressive in appearance, surprises you with its by-the-side-of-the-road friendliness and, in its own way, excellent food.

Inside the cafe, you share a long table or the counter and listen to whatever is being discussed. Something always is. You probably won't order the "Garbage Omelette," but should you be in such an adventurous mood, the girl behind the counter says, "It's got every-thing in it," starting with eight eggs.

"Does anybody ever eat a whole one?"

"Oh, sure," says the waitress. "A man was in here the other day and he ordered one for himself and one for his wife. He ate all his and half his wife's, too."

From Coburg, take Coburg Road North. In about a mile and a half is an historical marker noting that to the east, at the foot of the Coburg Hills — which climb to some 3000 feet — is where Joaquin (Cincinnatus Heiner) Miller, "poet of the Sierras," used to live as a boy. The Miller home is gone now, and a large, red farmhouse stands in its place. The current resident says he used the bricks from the original home's foundation to build his fireplace.

Miller, who in time would be lionized in London as the "Byron of Oregon," was a teenager when he lived here in the 1850s.

"He was a hippie," says a local resident. "Got in a lot of trouble in Eugene, then went over to Canyon City and they made him a judge." The "trouble" was probably over his secessionist leanings during the Civil War.

Keep driving north for another ten miles to the crossroads sign that points east to Diamond Hill Road. Take it to cross the I-5 over-pass. The road soon turns north again and wriggles through a wood-sy verge of the dark, forested foothills, then continues another ten miles to State Highway 228. You will likely stop to admire an old barn, perhaps to have a wayside picnic supplemented with wild blackberries.

It's better to take Highway 228 west to Halsey and go the rest of the way to Albany on 99E; this way you avoid coming into town the back way. Then take U.S. 20 west across the Willamette, and almost immediately after you have crossed the bridge, turn right onto Springhill Drive. It passes a golf course and goes through pretty farm country — fields hemmed 'round with trees and filbert and cherry orchards — and when you see the sign that tells you it's four miles to Buena Vista, you are on your way to a ferry ride.

A few houses hidden behind neglected old rosebushes are all there is left of Buena Vista, but ferry service here has gone on since 1851, when Reason B. Hall, who laid out the town, began operating

*The Buena Vista ferry gives free mini-voyages across
the Willamette River.*

"Hall's Ferry." He also named the place. During the Mexican War, some of his relatives had fought in the battle of Buena Vista. Besides, the town did have a beautiful view.

In his charming book, *Willamette Landings,* Howard McKinley Corning says that in 1870 Amedee Smith's pottery at Buena Vista had "four 'tyrners' and ten Chinese mixing clay." Smith's was the first stoneware plant in the Pacific Northwest; but when the pottery moved to Portland, and stage and railroad travel replaced water transportation, Buena Vista all but vanished.

The little ferry, however, still takes farmers and travelers back and forth across the Willamette's 1000 feet of water on a smooth, approximately four-minute, electrically operated cruise. The ferry runs, free of charge, from 7:00 a.m. until 8:50 p.m. every day except Saturdays, Sundays, and holidays, "when anybody wants across."

Buena Vista Park is a pleasant spot just above the ferry slip, with generous parking for cars and boat trailers. A handy boat launch lets you put in for a spot of fishing, and with luck, you'll take home some bass for supper.

An Albany couple leaves Buena Vista Park launching pad for an afternoon of bass fishing.

The back road to Salem parallels the freeway for about twelve miles and cuts through a corner of the Ankeny National Wildlife Refuge. Queen Anne's lace, rosy steeplebush, and wild roses grow in a tangle along the road, and birds chatter in the trees and fly back and forth across your path. It has been a good day puttering along, like a real trip, almost an excursion.

BROWNSVILLE: An Enchanting Small Town

Brownsville, Oregon's third-oldest town, is an enchanting place. Twenty-eight miles north of Eugene and across the Calapooia River, this peaceful community nudging the Cascade foothills is instant nineteenth century and charming. Its main street is full of turn-of-the-century buildings, some handsome brick structures with great arched doorways and tall windows, often with small plaques that tell something of their histories. Everywhere you meet with smiles from residents, who number about 1200.

"Yes, I guess we are pretty friendly here," says a clerk in a shop along Main Street. "We know most everybody here. It's kind of fun to have visitors."

Brownsville's early elegance is immediately visible as you come into town, for the Moyer House, an imposing "Italianate villa,"

*The Moyer House, open to visitors, recalls
Brownsville's more opulent days.*

faces directly on Main Street. With bay windows, elaborate cornices, porches, and balconies, and a third-story cupola, it is Brownsville's showplace. The house is beautifully kept up and is usually open to the public every afternoon but Monday during the summer. You are free to wander through its spacious rooms under twelve-foot ceilings. A guide is on hand to answer questions.

The large, square piano, velvet-upholstered chairs, and elaborate mantel clock above the marble fireplace are reminiscent of a gracious age when Brownsville was a leading city of Linn County — indeed, for a while in the beginning, the county seat. Above the high windows, formal landscapes are painted on glass panels, and similar scenes decorate the doors' old-fashioned transoms.

Be sure to visit the Linn County Historical Museum at 106 Spaulding Avenue — somehow the letter *u* got inserted in the name of the street, which was meant to honor Henry Spalding, a Presbyterian missionary who came to the Willamette Valley in 1836. The old railroad depot on Park Avenue, off Main Street, is being completely restored and eventually will house the museum's excellent collection of early-day mementos.

The museum's Victorian bedroom has a commode with decorative wash bowl and pitcher, and on its quilt-covered bed lie realistic figures of a mother and child pillowed against its high headboard. A lot of visitors ask Bill Lewis, the curator, "Are you sure you never sell any of these things? Can't you?" There's a beguiling collection of miniature vehicles, forty-nine of them meticulously hand-carved to scale, assembled, and painted by the late Willard H. Austin. Representative of the changing years, the tiny vehicles include a typical covered wagon in which the pioneers came across the plains, a twenty-mule-team wagon, a fringed tallyho, and, finally, a modern school bus.

Ask Lewis to explain the workings of the strange "piano player" — not, mind you, a "player piano." It is a rare contraption: the music roller is inserted into the piano player cabinet, which must be pulled up to the piano. When turned on, it strikes the piano keys with its own set of hammers. Pretty complicated — so much so that the invention failed to catch on. "Only two of them in the United States," says the curator.

Pick up a walking-tour guide at the museum. It will take you through Old Downtown, past the little millrace that once powered both grist and woolen mills, and alongside "carpenter-built" houses dating from the 1870s onward, including one in which Old Liza, said to have been the last member of the Calapooia Indian tribe, once lived. That name, by the way, seems to have been spelled a few dozen different ways, often Calapooya and even Kalapuya.

Shopping in Brownsville is pleasantly uncrowded in pretty, modern stores behind nineteenth-century facades. In a brick-walled former bank, now a fabric shop, the owner has transformed the old vault into a brightly lit and cozy office. The interior of the Citizens Valley Bank on Main Street is as old-fashioned as its brick exterior, with antique teller cages behind wood cabinetwork. Tall, etched-glass doors open into the Brownsville General Store. A sign on the front of the building calls it the oldest commercial establishment in town. Beneath its fourteen-foot ceilings you'll find everything from bulk grains to shining copper pieces.

The book *Brownsville,* by local historians Margaret Standish Carey and Patricia Hoy Hainline, offers colorful details about the town's beginnings. The book is sold all over Brownsville, and its anecdotes are sure to make your own discoveries more fun.

On most days the pace is leisurely in Brownsville, but late June is something else. To see the community in action, come to the annual Linn County Pioneer Picnic on the third weekend in June. It is the oldest continuing celebration in Oregon, and for three days it flows over into the ten-acre City Park, starting each morning with a wagon train breakfast.

The celebration is held near the spot where Alexander Kirk operated a ferry across the Calapooia starting in 1846. He bought his piece of land, it seems, from an even earlier settler for a yoke of oxen and a sturdy log chain. His ferry was a flatboat, hand-hauled across the stream by a rope.

Also in late June, the strangely twisted wisteria tree that graces the front lawn of Moyer House will be in full bloom. Some say that Old Liza braided its young limbs to form its convoluted trunk, but others insist that it was "Aunt Betty Moyer" herself, the original Mrs. Moyer of the fashionable villa and the daughter of Hugh L. Brown, for whom this inviting little town was named.

IS THIS THE ANDES?:
On the Trail with a Llama

An exotic sight has been added to the Oregon landscape these last few years. Sometimes on a trail in the Three Sisters Wilderness, other times on the slopes of Mount Hood, again among a herd of sheep, or just in the back forty of a farmer's lot — llamas! More and more you see these haughty, woolly creatures that most people associate only with the Andes. Not so anymore. Popular as pets and as the perfect pack animal, llamas have begun to appear all over the country, but nowhere as often as in Oregon, which is becoming known as the nation's "llama capital."

Why do you see llamas in a field of sheep? Because, explains Daniel Schoenthal — who, with his partners Tom and Toni Landis,

Aristocrats of wilderness trails, these llamas live quietly on their trainer's small farm.

operates Oregon Llamas for Unique Wilderness Travel — they chase the coyotes away. Wolves (virtually extinct in Oregon now), coyotes, and dogs are about the only animals that bother a llama, Schoenthal says. But the five-foot-tall llamas take off after those few pests without hesitation, and so, "they keep the coyotes away from the sheep."

In their traditional role as pack animals, llamas have proved so satisfactory on the trail that they are beginning to change the whole concept of pack trips, Schoenthal believes. They are sure-footed and intelligent, he says, gentle and quiet, and they can carry heavy loads all day without difficulty.

How do llamas compare with horses and mules on the trail? "There is no comparison," says the packer, who has had fifteen years' experience backpacking in the Oregon woods.

Horses are easily spooked. And a horse, says Schoenthal, "can do more damage to a trail than fifteen people can." A llama, with its even-toed, soft-padded feet, leaves less impression on a trail than a hiker's best hiking boot, says the expert. And its trail manners are exceptional — neat as a cat.

"Horses are flighty, and mules don't like tough ground. Llamas fit well in Oregon. They are good for rough country."

They are also easy to train, says Schoenthal, who has about twenty-five male llamas at his home on the outskirts of Albany, in the Willamette Valley. Here he trains them for use as pack animals and as pets for people who simply want a few of the exotic, shaggy characters looking down their elegant noses over the back fence. Under their white eyelashes!

Another pleasant fact: the llamas' thick wool has no oil and is therefore virtually odorless. Still, the greatest thing about having a llama carry your duds on a trail trip, Schoenthal insists, is that the llama enjoys the trek. Like a dog, "he gets excited about going along, and if you don't take him, he gets mad." That is, he gets miffed, his feelings hurt a bit. Also, adds Schoenthal, "They are amazingly healthy."

An adult llama can carry a load of 125 pounds, although 60 to 70 pounds is the average backpacking load — and none of that, as with a horse, is food for the pack animal. A llama is quite content to munch whatever is around. As a result, everyone has less to carry on his or her own back.

What is that yarn about how a llama can spit for thirty feet?

"They do spit when they're on the defensive," says the trainer, "just the way a dog bites under the same conditions. But a trained dog doesn't bite, and a trained llama doesn't spit."

Schoenthal tells how in the Andes a family group of one stud and from five to twenty females and their crias — their babies — live together in areas that have been used as home territories for 500 years. Bachelor herds, meanwhile, climb off into the mountains.

No llamas have been available from Peru and Bolivia since the 1930s, so the ones you see here were born in the United States. The International Llama Organization has held three of its annual conventions in Oregon; the 1982 meeting was held at Sun River. Schoenthal estimates that there are 4000 llamas in the United States, 1000 of them in Oregon.

The trainer-packer holds an open house for visitors to his Albany home on Sundays from 10:00 a.m. to 4:00 p.m. (His address is 2714 Riverside Drive South, Albany, Oregon 97321; call [503] 926-8443 for an appointment.) He will take you out to meet his llamas and no doubt tell you that on trail expeditions he likes a gourmet touch, including crepes for breakfast and campfire dishes stir-fried in a wok. He may even assure you that, "You won't eat as well on a cruise ship!"

A HOLIDAY FOR LIPS:
It's a Pucker-Up Event

Mitch Hider, who lives in the woods outside of Alpine, used to be a newspaperman — a good one — in San Francisco and in Salem. Then one day, "just for the heck of it," he and a friend entered a whistling contest in Carson City, Nevada.

There's been a cover on his typewriter ever since, and Hider has been whistling to delighted audiences all over Oregon. He puckers up at county fairs, at smelt-fry fetes and all kinds of other festivals, at special school doings, and frequently for senior citizens. He usually appears in a wizard suit and always accompanies himself with a little ukulele. His whistling is clear and sweet, and he manages a Verdi aria with the same apparent ease as his bird trills.

It's a funny thing how people who insist they can't whistle start trying when Hider is around. They pucker up and start blowing,

Whistler Mitch Hider shows a youngster how at the Holiday for Lips Festival.

and find they can do it. And this is exactly what happens every autumn at Hider's Holiday for Lips. This is a zany, offbeat fun-festival held every year on the first Saturday in November in the auditorium of the Benton County Fairgrounds at Corvallis — and it's free. It starts at eleven in the morning and continues until five that afternoon, and the crowd usually gets bigger and bigger as the day goes on.

No festival could be more informal, but this time Hider shows up in a tux. He uses a crazy lot of props, including the ukulele, of course, an old piano, a collection of drums, and a crystal goblet.

During the afternoon, a good many people who never intended to leave their seats find themselves up on stage with Hider, whose easy-going personality is the kind that inspires everybody else. Guests are welcome to bring their own music-making devices. Some come-back-every-year members of the audience appear with kazoos, bag-pipes, saws, bells, and bones, and one enthusiastic performer usually plays the spoons.

"It's all just a chance for everyone to have some fun," says the whistler.

The whistling master of ceremonies gives souvenir "whistler's lips" made of bright plastic to the first fifty performers who join him on stage, but every participant gets some kind of award. A gift awaits the first person who can laugh and whistle at the same time — usually somebody succeeds. But the one prize still waiting to be given away will go to the first performer who can shatter the goblet with his or her high-velocity whistling!

"The nice thing about whistling," says Hider, "is that we all pretty much understand how it's done. Mostly, though, we whistle for ourselves, so a Holiday for Lips is rather uncommon."

The maestro's Holiday for Lips is all of that and more.

"Last year's," says Hider, "was quite a blowout."

3
A Piece of the Southwest

Miles of good fishing spots on the North Umpqua are right off State Highway 138.

Southwestern Oregon has a special quality all its own. White-water buffs know it for the turbulent gorges of its wild and scenic river, the Rogue, and avid fishermen know it for its steelhead and salmon. Thousands of people visit Ashland for its annual theater season. Still the region's charm seems, if not quite unsung, at least not sung enough.

Visitors to the southwest corner of the state are treated to tumbling streams, historic gold towns, nearly traffic-free, mountain-rimmed back roads, and festivals ranging from Shakespeare to rooster crows.

SPRING WILDFLOWERS:
Beside the Tumbling Umpqua

It was in 1890, says Lewis A. McArthur in his *Oregon Geographic Names,* that the first postmaster of Glide found a name for that tiny settlement on the North Umpqua River. What should the place be called? she wondered. Then one day she heard her young son singing about how "the river goes gliding along."

But of course — Glide! What better name for a hamlet perched beside the dark green river that seems to glide along so purposefully? How distinctive the personalities of rivers: some lazy — unconcerned, it would seem — about where they are going; others downright confused, quite unable to make up their minds about which route to take; then those like the Umpqua, sure and authoritative.

Splashed with snowy riffles as it tumbles down from the Cascades, the Umpqua also attracts an authoritative breed of fisherman. In July and August you will see them, rubber-booted to the waist and ready for the summer steelhead, as worthy an opponent as any river provides. For thirty-two miles upstream from Rock Springs, the anglers' only lures will be flies.

Glide is still a small and quiet village stretched along the riverbanks. But on the third weekend in April, approximately 5000 people come visiting. State Highway 138 northeast out of Roseburg becomes a very busy thoroughfare as Glide presents its much-loved spring wildflower show. For nearly two decades the Glide Community Association has staged the event in its community hall just off the highway on Bug Farm Road, and year after year Oregonians return to admire what spring has brought forth again and to learn a bit of botany firsthand. About a dozen experienced pickers will have

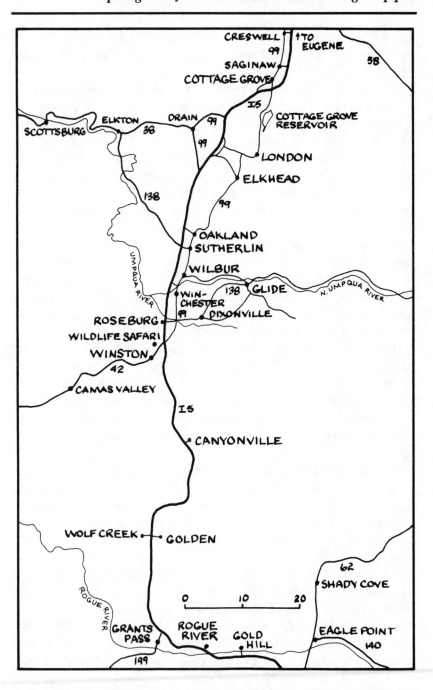

scoured the region from mountains to coast. Usually they collect at least 500 species of wildflowers that appear each spring in southwestern Oregon.

"We've picked in snow and in hot sun," says one of the women who searched field and bog, "and we've sloshed around in rubber boots."

By now the pickers are botanists in their own right, but just to be sure about both the Latin and common names for all of the plants, a botany professor is called upon to identify them. All kinds and colors of blossoms dotting April's emerald hills, creeks, and riverbanks are displayed on tables in the spacious hall. Many plants are growing in mossy dish gardens, some delicate miniatures even in tiny ashtrays.

The gleaming white dogwood petals are the showiest now; but the golden brooms, both Scotch and French, are worthy competitors, and so are the blue delphinium, the wild lilacs, and the red-flowering currant. There are salmonberry and thimbleberry, all manner of violets and shooting stars, and a myriad of tiny varieties that hide their modest blooms in deep grasses.

Mushrooms grow in a terrace of moss, and a surprising number of species are represented in a bed of lichens, including those tiny, red-tipped ones called "British soldiers." The British themselves pronounce the word as *litchens* — a cozier sound than our *likens,* isn't it? Samples of twigs and cones represent every conifer in the region, as well as some from other climes that have at one time or other flourished here.

"We have all kinds of trees planted on our new place," remarks a woman as she counts the five needles to a bundle on a branch of sugar pine. "We're up here to learn what we have." She points proudly to a spray of giant sequoia. "We even have one of those."

Ladies are serving sandwiches at a counter, and pies are spread on a table nearby.

"Oh, I'll take the gooseberry," says a visitor who knows his own mind, but with creamy chocolate, deep apple, coconut custard, mince, and pumpkin, decision making is difficult.

A delightful program of slides showing close-ups of western flowers is presented several times a day in a small auditorium in an adjoining building, and the expert's talk following the show weaves history, personal experience, and technical detail without once sounding didactic.

The wildflower show opens each morning from eight to nine o'clock for photographers, and after that visitors may stroll in and out of the hall for the rest of the day. There is no charge, but donations are accepted.

If you came by Highway 138 from Roseburg, vary the way back by taking the seventeen-mile, unnumbered but smoothly paved, two-lane road between Glide and Wilbur. It runs close to the river through roller-coaster hills where black-faced sheep graze along the hillsides. Sometimes the sun seems to have spilled over onto the open fields, so gold are their buttercups, or the sky to have fallen, leaving broad patches of pastel blue. One understands why Lewis and Clark, coming across swathes of blue camas like these, thought they were looking at lakes.

THE BACK WAY:
Historic Towns and Apple Pie

When you are heading south for Ashland — that is, Shakespeare Town — during its annual eight-month metamorphosis from farm community into Stratford-on-Avon, why not go the pleasant back way?

The "Old Highway" 99 can be your main route for most of the way, and what a relief from the crowded freeway! Either 99E or 99W — east or west of the Willamette River — will take you from Portland to Eugene. Then Highway 99 (no longer are there east and west branches) weaves south, sometimes as a frontage road for small towns off Interstate 5, sometimes merging with the interstate for a few miles.

Drive the twenty miles south from Eugene to Cottage Grove on Highway 99; then be adventurous and continue via London. Simply stay on the highway through Cottage Grove until you see the sign for London Road. Take it.

London Road runs close beside the blue waters of Cottage Grove Reservoir. Traffic is virtually nil, and logging trucks are no problem, for they have their own road parallel to yours. Weekend farmers live around here, probably commuters who simply want to "live in the country." And London? A handful of houses and a charming, white, steepled Baptist Church. No one seems to have any idea why this hamlet was named London. Do you remember Edna St. Vincent Millay's poem about the road "too lovely to explore" that led only to "the milk-man's door"? Perhaps it's more fun not to know.

If you do the natural thing in London and follow the pavement's yellow line, you end in a farmer's yard. So look for the Shoestring Road sign at the corner across from the church. Shoestring Road leads over London Hill, and it doesn't matter, does it, that it's not paved, when it has such a nice name? The hill is forested with Douglas fir and is steep and winding, but it's your own private route. Five miles later a sign will direct you to Oakland, which is another nineteen seldom-if-ever-interrupted and delightful miles. Though nothing indicates it, you will go through Elkhead, which used to be called Shoestring.

Sheep graze on tilted hills, and mustard blossoms turn the fields to gold. Clusters of mistletoe, like huge birds' nests, crowd the branches of the big Oregon oaks, after which Oakland was named.

If Oakland is new to you, you'll be surprised by the fancifully ornamented buildings on the main street. Oakland used to be a major stop for the California Stage Line in the 1850s. The original town was just north of its present location, close to a convenient ford on Calapooia Creek. It was a busy town, particularly the one day a week when the mail came in. Saddle and pack horses were lined up at the post office to hurry the mail off to Eugene and to Corvallis — then Marysville — to Scottsburg on the Umpqua River, and south to Jacksonville.

When the Oregon and California Railroad ran its rails south of town in 1872, Oaklanders simply jacked up their houses, harnessed their teams, and moved the town. And when its wooden buildings burned in the 1890s, again the residents got out their teams, hauled in local brick and hand-cut stone, and rebuilt the town — and with what imposing decor! High, arched windows, tall chimneys, and

European-style masks ornament downtown buildings in Oakland.

odd little cement masks attached to cornice corners are pretty fancy for a sleepy Oregon farm town's Main Street. Still, this elegance of another day confers a certain stateliness on the street, where pickup trucks are parked at the curb.

Tolly's will surprise you, too. The restaurant is located midway along Main Street, with tubs of flowers out front. Stop for lunch or a snack, a milkshake at the long bar, or a draught of beer or wine amid the greenery of plants in the loft. The brick-walled restaurant offers a slightly overwhelming array of pies, cakes, breads, bagels, and buns, as well as candies and gifts, and shares space under its high ceilings with an adjoining antique shop.

Highway 99 heads south from Oakland through Sutherlin and Wilbur to Roseburg. There is nothing in Wilbur to remind you of the Reverend James H. Wilbur, who came around the Horn to Oregon in 1846, but he was one of Oregon's early leading educators. His goal was to open preparatory schools for Willamette University, established at Salem in 1853.

For some years, Umpqua Academy in Wilbur was the only seat of "higher learning" between Sacramento and Salem. Its announced

purpose was "to form correct mental and moral habits, and to culti-
vate a taste for intellectual pursuits." Regulations forbade "profane,
obscene or vulgar language or unchaste yarns or narratives, or im-
moral gestures or hints." "Night reveling" was out, too. Father
Wilbur, as he was called, must be turning in his grave.

Where Highway 99 crosses the low falls of the Umpqua River,
note the long row of steps down to the stream at the north end of the
bridge. They lead to a tiny concrete hut built into the water, where
the salmon coming upstream are counted during seasonal runs. You
could hardly get a closer look, though fleeting — the fish move along
at a no-nonsense pace. Sometimes a long, slim eel swims by to vary
the show.

Across the Umpqua is one of Oregon's most attractive county
parks — Douglas County's John P. Amacher Park. It is spacious and
shady and has fine fishing, a launching dock, fireplaces, and show-
ers, making it a comfortable place to camp or stop for a picnic.

Roseburg, about five miles south of the park, is a pretty city set in
its bowl of hills beside the splashing Umpqua. Douglas County seat,
the city was established in 1851 by Aaron Rose, and it was named
for him. General Joseph Lane, Oregon's first territorial governor,
lived here, and his former home is now one of the area's historical
landmarks.

The 1940 Public Works Administration guide to Oregon recalls
that Roseburg city fathers passed an extraordinary ordinance in
1899 prohibiting the use of bells on cows. One Roseburg citizen who
liked to get his full quota of sleep began removing the bells from
local cows and tossing them into the gutter. The ordinance must
have pleased him. It decreed that no bells be used on cows or any
domestic animals between the hours of 8:00 p.m. and 6:00 a.m.

From Roseburg you have the choice of swinging west on Highway
99 to Winston, home of Oregon's Wildlife Safari, or taking to the
freeway for a spell. Either way, it's not far to Mexia's, and that's an
important stop.

If you know Mexia's memorable pies, served in a small house just
off the pike south of Canyonville, you know the place is a mecca for
pie lovers. But when you're driving south, the small cafe is a bit
tricky to locate. A garage man on Canyonville's main street knows

the directions by heart. He is explaining to a tourist, who, map in hand, has asked, "This is Canyonville, isn't it?"

"Sure is!" cries the friendly mechanic in a bellow easily heard across the street.

"Somebody up in Portland," begins the traveler, "was telling me about some place here where the pies were —"

"Mexia's!" shouts the mechanic. "Right up the hill there in the trees — you won't see it till you get there. Been there more'n half a century. Get back on the freeway," he advises, pointing a greasy finger, "and take the first exit, about two miles. You'll see the overpass, and it'll bring you back across the highway. Then turn right and just keep going till you see the house. Only one there. That's Mexia's, and you'll probably smell the pies before you get there."

That is, indeed, the way to Mexia's. Later, full of pie and contentment, you're ready to continue southward; so head back along

Loson Winn has been serving Mexia's plump pies since 1927.

the frontage road into Canyonville to get back onto the freeway. Driving north, there's no trouble. You see the little house with its big sign as you come to the exit.

Although her pies have won her acclaim, Mexia is something of a myth; she rarely appears in the front room where her husband, Loson Winn, serves guests at four small tables. Winn is a handsome octogenarian; a picture of him in full Masonic uniform hangs among dozens of commemorative plates on the walls.

"I've been in business here since 1927," he says. "I built the house five years before that. My wife bakes the pies."

Should you be fortunate enough to meet the artist in the kitchen, she may tell you that she used to bake forty to fifty pies a day — now a dozen or so is about average.

"But we're not ready to quit," she says.

When asked for her secret — her pies are on a magical plane not of this world — her black eyes twinkle. "Practice," she replies.

People write to Mexia asking for recipes. "I usually mix three pounds of shortening at a time — I couldn't tell anybody how . . . "

Mexia's pies follow the seasons: Satsuma plum, perhaps, on an April menu, berries in summer, pumpkin in season, and always, every day, apple. The cafe has sandwiches and hamburgers, too, but the pies are what keep customers coming back again and again. Hours are from noon to 4:00 p.m. on weekdays and Sundays except during salmon season, when the Winns always close down on Fridays and Saturdays and go off to Winchester Bay to fish.

Highway 99 merges with I-5 for most of the way to Grants Pass, approximately the old stage route of the 1860s. Canyonville was a coach stop and so was Wolf Creek, twenty miles to the south. By 1860 the Oregon and California Stage Company was carrying mail and passengers between "Sacramento City" and Portland. The trip took six days.

Harold A. Minter tells about the smart Concord coaches in his 1967 book *Umpqua Valley Oregon and its Pioneers*. They were painted gold with olive green trim, and all traffic stopped for them. No wonder, for a coach, Minter says, was drawn by six white horses in shining black harness "trimmed with silver buckles and ivory rings."

Wolf Creek Tavern takes you back to the last century, but dining there is up to date and splendid.

Each coach carried nine passengers inside and nine outside, on the top. When winter rains came, similar vehicles stripped down to basics replaced the elegant ones. Mud wagons, they were called, and when the mud got too deep, passengers had to get out and help push. True northwestern spirit.

Wolf Creek Tavern, located a mile off the freeway in the town of Wolf Creek, once again caters to travelers as it did during the 1870s. Now on the National Register of Historic Places, the hostelry was originally built between 1868 and 1873. The gracious, two-story, white frame building with its balcony across the front looks very much like pictures of the original tavern, as such inns were called then.

Over the decades various owners have changed the interior: adding a south wing, enlarging the bedrooms, and installing modern baths throughout. Now owned by the state, the inn is leased to

Vernon and Donna Wiard. Its ladies' parlor, men's tap room, and eight bedrooms are furnished to represent different periods during the inn's history. The attractively restored parlor chambers upstairs are the most fun; the downstairs rooms, with their skimpy rugs and sparse furnishings — no doubt a faithful representation — can leave guests less than enchanted with pioneer life. The meals at the inn are really excellent, pleasantly served by costumed waitresses, and, like the rooms, moderately priced. Reservations usually need to be made for either rooms or dinner. Write to Wolf Creek Tavern, P.O. Box 97, Wolf Creek, Oregon 97497, or call (503) 866-2474.

If you like to collect ghost towns, take the Coyote Creek Road east for four miles from Wolf Creek to Golden, a settlement once most appropriately named. When prospectors first found gold scattered throughout the gravels of Coyote Creek, they filed claims there, one right next to another. When the miners heard about the Salmon River diggings in Idaho, however, they picked up their shovels and left. It took no time at all, then, for some 500 Chinese to take over all the abandoned claims. Once the Idaho gold played out, the miners returned and hastily pushed out the Chinese.

In the 1890s Golden was a reversal of human nature — it had two churches and no saloons. The Reverend William Ruble built a Campbellite church in 1892, and another Ruble, probably his son, ran the general store. Ruble's church, rebuilt in 1950, is an appealing one, its belfry reaching into the branches of an overhanging tree. The church, the old store, and a tall derelict of an unfinished building are about all that's left of Golden. An old blackboard on

This historical society sign highlights the history of Golden during the days when "color" shone in the creek.

Golden's Community Church was built circa 1852.

the church porch lists "Sunday school at 10 — Preaching at 11," but a sign in larger letters under a window simply reads "For Sale." Just beyond the store, a large sign put up by the Josephine County Historical Society notes the highlights of Golden's past, and up on the mountain an occasional prospector still washes color out of Coyote Creek.

Interstate 5 curls up and down forested hills for twenty miles to Grants Pass. From here Highway 99 edges the green Rogue River for about another twenty miles, joins the freeway briefly, then runs parallel to Bear Creek past pear and apple orchards the twenty-nine miles to Medford and another twelve miles to Ashland.

The Three Oaks Country Store, between Grants Pass and the town of Rogue River, is a charming place to stop for lunch or a coffee break. It is at 6801 Rogue River Highway, which is what Highway 99 is called here. The old farmhouse, built in 1859, is the second oldest in Josephine County. It's spanking white, and the original outside stairway is still intact. When James and Margaret Savage arrived at this spot above the Rogue by covered wagon, Margaret is said to have asserted, "We've gone far enough." They stayed. Eventually they built the house that is now the Country Store, and they raised thirteen children. The nearby Savage Dam is named for the family.

Lunches inside or outside at umbrella-shaded tables are good and comfortably priced. The Country Store is closed on Mondays.

ROGUE RIVER:
Something To Crow About

On the last Saturday in June every year, Rogue River stages one of Oregon's zaniest festivals — the Rogue River Rooster Crow. It has been going on since 1953, when a local merchant read about rooster-crowing contests in Wales. The gimmick is to see how many times a rooster will crow during a thirty-minute period.

Kenny Koral presents Rooster Crow winning cock, Crow-In Joe.

In the first Rogue River contest, Hollerin' Harry crowed 71 times and won his young owner fifty dollars. Since then, the festival has grown to include a parade, races, an arts and crafts show, an old-car exhibit, and square dances, but the crowing session is the day's high point. Sixty or 70 crows are about average for most of the cocks, but in 1978 White Lightning forged ahead with 112 decisive statements. The cocky champion's record has yet to be bested.

When White Lightning's proud owner was asked about his training method, he explained that he had kept the rooster away from any other rooster or chicken for six weeks before the contest. White Lightning obviously was the gregarious type.

JACKSONVILLE:
Nostalgia the Theme

"If I could retire right now, I think I'd like to live in Jacksonville."

That's a remark often made by visitors to this charming old town in southern Jackson County. In fact, a good many of Jacksonville's 2000 residents are retirees. The town is a bit off the main track, and nostalgia is its predominant quality. The gold rush days are a continuing interest — after all, gold built the town.

It was in the winter of 1851-52 that James Cluggage and James Poole, prospecting along a small tributary of Jackson Creek, found gold in their pans. Almost overnight thousands of miners arrived, many coming up from California in hopes of finding richer deposits. Within weeks Jacksonville had become a boom town, and soon it became the first seat of Jackson County. A marker at Oak and Applegate streets shows the location of that first gold discovery in Oregon.

The gold lasted only a few years, and as it disappeared, Jacksonville's exuberance faded. The railroad bypassed the town in 1884, and by 1927 Jacksonville reluctantly gave up the county seat to Medford. Still, it never became a ghost town. During the depression of the 1930s, gold fever broke out all over the place again. Men dug up their own backyards and washed the dirt through sluice boxes and rockers. Novus Webb of Jacksonville wrote that "the ringing of the blacksmith anvils" began each day as home-style miners had their picks and drills sharpened. For some there was just enough shiny stuff to live on during those jobless days; for others there was quite a bit. Right in the middle of town, at California and 4th streets, two men are said to have unearthed gold worth $25,000. Tunnels honeycombed the ground close beside St. Joseph's Catholic Church. Indeed, so many tunnels and shafts were dug throughout the town that for years cave-ins were a problem.

In time, artists and craftsmen began settling here; they liked the peaceful atmosphere. Now Jacksonville is a National Historic Landmark, and many of its handsome old brick buildings and Victorian houses have been repaired and refurbished. A lot of the oldest and most interesting buildings are on California Street and on nearby side streets.

The most impressive building on California is the old United States Hotel, which opened with great fanfare in 1880 to welcome President Rutherford B. Hayes as its first guest. The United States National Bank of Oregon operates here and, with its old gold scales and nineteenth-century paraphernalia, manages still to look like a bank of the 1880s.

Across the street at 3rd and California, the old Beekman Bank, which opened in 1863, has been left exactly as it was when the bank closed in 1912. Through its windows you see the old-fashioned furnishings, the wooden counters and the big, old desk and well-worn office chair of Owner C. C. Beekman.

The J. W. McCully Building at Oregon and Main streets has been a landmark since about 1855, when two feet of dirt was placed between roof and ceiling. You may be told that this was done in case Indians attacked with flaming arrows — and perhaps the builders really did think such a precaution was warranted. But no Indians ever shot flaming arrows into Jacksonville. So legends grow. Actually, in those days it was customary to insulate the roof of a commercial building with dirt so that it would not catch fire from the sparks from a nearby burning building. For years now the McCully Building has been headquarters for an Odd Fellows lodge. The Brunner

This pretty little Episcopal Church was originally built for the Methodists in 1854. It was the first Protestant church west of the Rockies.

Building across the street is another old-timer dating from 1855 or 1856.

It was a lucky night at the gaming tables, they say, that helped build the charming, white-steepled church at 5th and D streets for the Methodists in 1854. The oldest church building south of the Willamette Valley, it is now St. Andrew's Episcopal Church.

A block away, at 4th and D streets, is tall-spired St. Joseph's Roman Catholic Church, built in 1858 and dedicated by the famous Archbishop F. N. Blanchet. F. Y. Blanchet, the archbishop's nephew, was the pastor here from 1863 to 1877.

The sun still glows in the stained-glass windows of the First Presbyterian edifice at 6th and California. The windows were brought around the Horn in 1881. The church was built of sugar pine hauled by wagon the 100 miles or so from Roseburg. Sunday services are still held at all three churches.

The sweetest building of all is the modest cottage that used to be the Catholic rectory. Behind its white picket fence, it is beautifully kept up by the Southern Oregon Historical Society and is open to visitors from noon to 4:30 p.m. every day throughout the summer. The cherrywood grandfather's clock, tall and imposing in a corner

*The Jacksonville Inn maintains last century charm,
twentieth-century comfort, and sophisticated cuisine.*

of the small parlor, was made sometime before 1820 and brought
across plains and mountains by covered wagon. From iron heating
stove to melodeon, the furnishings are antiques, some of them from
the former home of Jacksonville's first leading artist, Peter Britt.
The melodeon had something of a checkered career. Once, its lid
firmly down, it had doubled as a butcher's block!

To be sure, Jacksonville has its shoppes tailored for the tourist in a
hurry, but it also has some fine antique stores, such as Scheffel's on
West California, and a number of delightful art galleries. The lovely paintings of nationally acclaimed artist Eugene Bennett are on
display in his gallery at 355 South Oregon Street.

Jacksonville has chosen not to become clogged with motels, so
most overnighters stop in Medford. The Jacksonville Inn, however,
is old but neatly renovated. Its eight rooms retain a nineteenth-
century appeal but with modern baths, and the chill is removed
with baseboard heat. The continental fare served in the brick-
walled dining room is splendid — seven-course dinners are featured,
as well as a fine wine list. Reservations are usually necessary; write to
the Jacksonville Inn, 175 East California Street, Jacksonville, Oregon 97530, or telephone (503) 889-8807.

A couple of favorite luncheon places are Plymale Cottage, at 180 North Oregon Street, and the Bella Union, 170 West California Street. The cottage, a restored home of the 1860s, has a modern tearoom ambiance, with pretty papered walls and prints, pretty dishes on flowered tablecloths, and some old collectables for sale, too.

The Bella Union reflects its beginnings as the Bella Union Saloon, founded in 1856 and rebuilt after a fire in 1874. Here, red-and-white-checkered tablecloths set the tone, while a huge mirror against the brick wall and a long, long bar and mural of early-day Jacksonville catch the flavor of the town in its horse-and-buggy days. A garden courtyard roofed over with a great wisteria vine is inviting on a summer's day — but get there early; it's small and popular.

Every visitor should tour the Jacksonville Museum in the stately old courthouse at 206 North 5th Street. There are museums and museums, but Jacksonville's is exceptional, and free. The nineteenth-century Italianate building was constructed in 1884, and it served as the county courthouse for forty-three years. Now it makes an ideal setting for the memorabilia of a gold town. Exhibits recall the pig-tailed Chinese who came to work the gold tailings, as well as the early white settlers — sheriff and judge, Wells Fargo agent and gambler, circuit rider and prospector, and their lace-gowned women. (There's nothing about Sally Stanford, who grew up in Jacksonville, but that was later anyway.)

Much is reminiscent of Peter Britt, Jacksonville's Renaissance man of the last century. Britt was a Swiss who came here in 1852. As a painter, photographer, vintner, and horticulturist, he made a name both for himself and for Jacksonville. He used to ride patiently by horse and buggy deep into the Cascades to record what he saw on glass-plate negatives and to paint mountainscapes. He was the first to photograph Crater Lake. As a memorial, Jacksonville's annual music festival is named for Peter Britt, and it is held in the old gardens of his once considerable estate.

The museum has set up Britt's photography studio as it was in his home. His huge, unwieldy cameras are focused on a small, round, marble-topped table and two elaborately fringed chairs, ready for clients. The Britts' home burned down, but the museum has re-

*The former Jackson County Courthouse is now
one of Oregon's finest historical museums.*

assembled its parlor, with its square Steinway piano, dark green velvet, serpentine-back sofa, and Louis XV chairs, circa 1865. The gas lamps had been electrified in 1910, the same year that the Beekman Bank acquired its modern lighting. Two of the room's large paintings in heavy, gilt frames are Britt's work; one is of Crater Lake.

Exhibits on the second floor belie the idealized image that has evolved of the western settler. Among the displays of primitive tools used by the Chinese to work the tailings left by white miners is a note written by one Chinese leader. He believed at first, he said, that "only the Irish" were opposed to the Chinese. But he had come to realize that everyone in the country wanted to restrict them and "prevent" others from coming in. Should any "massacres" occur, he warned, reprisals against "all foreigners" would also take place in China. Nothing could more clearly reveal the white miners' attitude in gold camps throughout Oregon.

This mural in the Children's Museum makes you believe you are really looking out the window.

The delightful Children's Museum is next door to the courthouse in the old jail. Eye-opening for youngsters and charming for adults, it, too, is free. "Touch gently" reads a sign, and everything in a series of lifelike settings depicting southwestern Oregon's history is for touching.

Artist Norman Campbell painted such convincing three-dimensional background murals for these displays that each small room feels remarkably true to life. Outdoor scenes painted between real window frames attached to the walls make you feel that you are actually looking outside.

The settings begin with a Takelman (Rogue River) Indian house and then move through the decades into this century. Wagon wheels and a piece of canvas against the wall give a vivid impression of a covered wagon. Small hands reach into the little trunk that was carried in the wagon to find a battered silver brush and mirror set, a treasure one pioneer could not bear to leave behind.

Young visitors crank the telephone on the wall and turn the handle of the big butter churn. They have a go at *McGuffey's Eclectic Primer* in the little schoolroom, and they try the pump at the wooden sink. In the upstairs loft, a general store has small but real bolts of cloth on its shelves. There are a shoeshiner's chair to sit in, a telephone switchboard to plug in and out, and all manner of labels to read on the drugstore's bottles: "Phenix 5¢ for your nerves"; "Drink Metto 5¢."

The loft also houses Pinto's Theater, where puppet shows are given on Tuesdays and Saturdays the summer long. Pinto? Pinto Colvig grew up in Jacksonville and later became the well-known Bozo the Clown. During the 1930s Pinto created the voices for Walt Disney's Mickey Mouse and Silly Symphony cartoons, and later for such familiar Disney characters as Pluto, Grumpy, Sleepy, and others. The clown often came back to Jacksonville to visit, and in 1963, four years before his death, he served as grand marshal of the Jacksonville Jubilee parade. Now, carrying on the tradition, a new clown named Pinto entertains in the museum theater.

If pioneer cemeteries are to your liking, Jacksonville's is old, peaceful, and spacious. On a broad hillside under the benevolent shade of a magnificent grove of madrone trees, the aging, white tombstones are streaked with black. Dates on the stones in a family plot often begin in the 1860s and continue into this century. The epitaphs and elegies are in a florid language not of our day. A daughter at "15 years, 9 months, 6 days," was "a bud of promise transplanted to Bloom in Heaven," while on another stone bereavement is simply enough expressed: "Thou hast made Heaven more necessary." Hours can pass unnoticed here.

Neglected tomb-stones in Jacksonville's Pioneer Cemetery recall a more florid day.

There's music in the hills during Jacksonville's annual Peter Britt Festival.

Music lovers will find Jacksonville most inviting in August, when the Peter Britt Music Festival draws enthusiastic crowds. The programs are presented out-of-doors in the gardens above Britt's former home. The first concerts were given in 1963, with the orchestra playing in a temporary enclosure, but since 1978 the musicians have performed in a large wooden pavilion.

Audiences assemble on the hillside — some on benches, some on folding chairs, most on cushions and car blankets on the grass — to hear Bach and Beethoven, Mozart and Mendelssohn, Handel and Haydn, and other classical masters. Founder-director John Trudeau assembles a fine orchestra for the two-week series, along with internationally known soloists and guest conductors. Recitals are also given in the upstairs ballroom of the old United States Hotel.

For information about the festival, as well as for the Blues and Country Music Festival in July and the Jazz Festival in August, write to the Britt Music Festival, P.O. Box 1124, Medford, Oregon 97501.

LOOP TRIP:
Wine Tasting and a Ghost Town

Late spring is a lovely time in southwestern Oregon. The leaves of the red-limbed madrone trees glisten in the sun, dogwood sprinkles the woods with its greenish-white blossoms, and wildflowers color the road banks. Horseback riders take to country roads, for this is horse country, and white picket fences surrounding pastures where fine horses graze are a familiar part of the landscape.

On a short loop trip out of Jacksonville along the Applegate River, there's a vineyard to visit, a lazy park for fishing, swimming, and picnicking, and a mysterious, small ghost town called Buncom to speculate about. Explorer-pioneer Lindsay Applegate prospected along the river in 1848, and they named it for him.

Take Highway 238 — the Medford-Provolt Highway — south to Ruch; then take Applegate Road and stop for a taste of wine at the Valley View Vineyard at 1000 Applegate Road. No European-style chateau here yet, but a lot of informal hospitality at the former pole barn the Wisnovsky family turned into a winery. Bonnie Morell is the one offering glasses of such Valley View specialties as Chardonnay, Gewürztraminer, and Cabernet Sauvignon.

Peter Britt planted the first Valley View Vineyard in 1854. The new one was started in 1971 with twenty-five acres of vinifera grapes; but the vineyard has eighty acres along the mountain-rimmed valley floor, and plans are to expand.

"Come around at harvest time," Bonnie urges. "That's when all the neighbors come to help harvest. It's great."

Visiting hours are from 11:00 a.m. to 5:00 p.m., mid-April through December, from 1:00 p.m. to 5:00 p.m. on winter weekends, or by appointment.

Farther south on Applegate Road is wonderfully woodsy McKee Bridge Park. Wildflowers poke their heads up through the grasses in

A sandy beach beside the Applegate River at McKee Park.

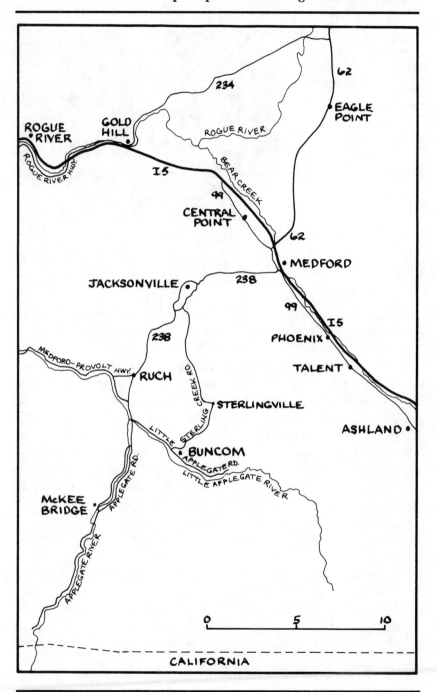

At the Sterling Creek Road sign, this dilapidated house stirs the imagination.

the shade of tall ponderosa pine and alder. Small wooden bridges arc across rivulets that snake down to sandy stretches beside the Applegate. The hill on the other side of the river seems to go straight up from the bubbling green water. You can't camp here, but there's picnicking at tables and rock fireplaces spaced well apart. The white covered bridge over the river, built in 1917 and no longer used, adds a bit of nostalgic charm.

On the way back to Jacksonville, turn onto Sterling Creek Road along the Little Applegate River. California poppies brighten the roadsides, hawks fly overhead, and red-winged blackbirds whir out of copses. Then, at a turn in the road, there is Buncom, a mysterious village that has a handful of dilapidated shacks to spur the imagination.

A fair stand of grass grows on the roof of — what? A battered stable?

A man on a bicycle stops to offer his opinion: "I think that one with the false front was a store."

Moss grows in the cracks, but the chimney is intact. The door is gone, and inside are jumbled stacks of rotting boards.

Across the road, broken pieces of a stove lie amid a tangle of flowering shrubs.

"Must have been a house there once. Japanese quince doesn't grow wild."

The cyclist begins talking about how great these wide, paved roads are for cycling.

"I can take off anytime," he says, "and ride for fifteen miles. No traffic, no trouble. I say how peaceful it is, and people in Ruch look at me as though they thought I was crazy. 'It's crowded!' they say." He laughs. "Just what I used to say in Marin County."

Sterling Creek Road goes back to town. Throughout the valley long piles of unearthed rock — placer tailings — appear along the streams, for the gold miners not only gouged out the banks of the Applegate but of all its tributary creeks as well. Still, clumps of willow and manzanita and alder climb through the rock crevices, slowly healing the scars.

It is beautiful coming into Jacksonville, that sleepy town of handsome trees and tall church spires. The loop trip covered about sixty miles, a pleasant sampling of a lovely countryside.

SHAKESPEARE TOWN: The Play's the Thing

Ashland is one of Oregon's most appealing small communities, so sweetly set in a hill-encircled hollow, with the Siskiyous high on its southern rim. It is a pretty town, with Lithia Park's lush gardens, the Southern Oregon State College campus, and gingerbread houses with filigree-carved balconies and old-fashioned roses clambering over arched trellises.

A quarter of a million people come to Ashland every year for the Shakespearean Festival that runs from late February through October. The fete's late founder-director, Angus L. Bowmer, staged the first Shakespearean plays here in 1935 in the old Chautauqua shell. Costumes were stitched together from relics out of Ashland attics, and the thespian talent was entirely local. Bowmer had persuaded reluctant city officials to grant him $400 in expenses, provided the stage were used for boxing matches during the day. The city fathers thought that the matches would make up for the theatrical losses. Instead, the plays covered the boxing losses.

Now fine actors from all over the nation present both Shakespearean and contemporary plays on the outdoor Elizabethan stage, the 600-seat Angus Bowmer Theater, and in the intimate Black Swan.

The bed-and-breakfast idea has taken hold in Ashland, and nearly a dozen houses offer down-comforter coziness and breakfasts to last the day. Ranging from two upstairs rooms in a private home to fairly elaborate accommodations, they add a touch of European hospitality to a town where banners emblazoned with royal arms wave high above the streets, and where even a brass-rubbing center seems to belong.

The Chamber of Commerce (P.O. Box 606) will provide a list of bed-and-breakfast places. For play schedules, write to the Oregon Shakespearean Festival, Ashland, Oregon 97520.

4
Just Over the Pass

The Metolius hurries out from under the ponderosa pines on Black Butte. Mount Jefferson stands tall in the distance.

From British Columbia to northern California, the Cascades march north-south in a chain of snow-crested peaks, and except for the group of mountains that crowd in friendly togetherness west of Bend, they are remarkably evenly spaced. This mountain cluster — the Three Sisters, Broken Top, and Bachelor Butte — attracts visitors year-round. They come in the hot, dry seasons to fish spring-fed mountain streams and to hike trails through alpine meadows to high-country tarns and lakes. In winter they can't seem to get here fast enough — hoping, and usually finding, that the rains moving through the Willamette Valley have become snow on Bachelor's ski slopes.

These serene-looking mountains, all above 9000 feet, were born of fierce volcanic activity. One day, geologists believe, that fiery violence may be renewed. In his book *Fire and Ice, The Cascade Volcanoes,* Stephen L. Harris points out that since the last Ice Age there has been "at least one major outburst per century among the Cascades," and that the Three Sisters area "is as likely as any . . . to stage a spectacular volcanic renaissance." He notes, however, that volcanoes usually offer warnings before they blow, and that when they do erupt they generally "begin on a small, harmless scale." Other than the fumaroles on Bachelor's northern slopes, the Three Sisters region has given no recent signs of possibly turning belligerent, and the entire area continues to be one of the most delightful playgrounds in all of Oregon's famed outdoors.

The change from west to east side of the Cascades is startling. No matter how well you know that the "other side" of the mountains will be different, you're always struck by the sudden contrast between the alpine fir and mountain hemlock atop a nearly 5000-foot-high pass like the Santiam and the parklike forest of ponderosa pines on its eastern side. A sudden contrast comes again a few miles farther east, where the pines give way to juniper and sagebrush. So let's come down past the blue waters of Suttle Lake into pine country, where the sun turns the cinnamon trunks of the ponderosas to bronze. Let's sample the seasons beside a swift mountain stream, visit a once-sleepy lumber town gone over to tourists and second-home residents, and have an elegant repast at a quiet restaurant, its ambiance more like that of Paris than of a mid-Oregon lumber town.

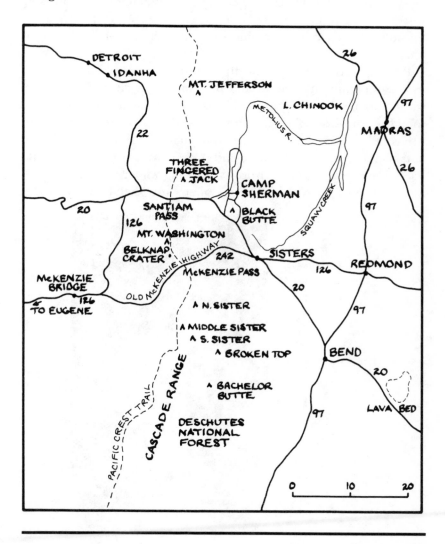

THE METOLIUS:
A Stream Like No Other

The swift little Metolius, one of the fastest-flowing rivers in the West, pours out of the ground at the foot of Black Butte's 6436-foot, forested cinder cone as though it had waited eons to emerge into the light. A stream like no other, it comes purring, chuckling — a dozen voices talking to one another — and curling up white as it pushes through a greenery of mimulus and water grasses and slides over rocks.

Rushing as though it can hardly wait to see the world, the Metolius passes mountain meadow and pine forest, its clear waters flush with its banks. Twisting around grassy bends, it hurries by small, round, stump-sized islands, where the wild grass grows so long that it has fallen over, making the islands look like miniature African huts. On past a fallen pine here and there, where trout hide in dark pools, the river races under bridges, growing wilder until it becomes a torrent. Swollen with the waters of streams that flow down the

A young fisherman over from Eugene has had a good morning on the Metolius.

It's a cagey river. They are down there, those rainbows, but will they or won't they?

eastern slopes of the Cascades — from Three Fingered Jack and Mount Jefferson — it swings eastward in a wide curve and, in a dramatic finale, rushes through a rugged gorge into Billy Chinook Lake to merge with the waters of the Deschutes and Crooked rivers.

A sweet mountain stream, the Metolius. It was called *Myptolas* by the Indians who knew it first, Matoles by early settlers, and now — apparently evolved from the rhythmic melody of the syllables — Metolius.

A small community a couple of miles from the river's source calls the Metolius its own. Camp Sherman is the locale of "The Store," which caters to the needs of some 100 families who have houses beside the stream, held by tenuous permission from the Deschutes National Forest Service. The congenial store and adjoining post office, with its antique post boxes, are the general meeting places for all. Up the road are a small chapel, an attractive two-room school, a trailer park, and some cabins for rent. Others are farther back from the river, where meadows open onto fantastic views of Cascade peaks — Mount Jefferson always the most visible and imposing.

The community's name came naturally enough. In an earlier day, after wheat farmers in hot Sherman County had brought in the harvest, they would trundle down to this far corner of Jefferson

Below the Camp Sherman bridge the lunkers lie, waiting patiently for crumbs.

County to camp beside the cold waters of the Metolius. The place became known as Camp Sherman, and the name stuck.

In those early days, mail used to be brought in by a team, and groceries were sold on an open platform, later covered by a tent, and eventually replaced by a small building. In 1949, when the late Katherine Smith, then postmaster, and her husband, Clarence, refinished the old building's interior, they found newspapers used as insulation under the floorboards. In one paper there was a picture of the gown Mrs. Woodrow Wilson had worn at her wedding.

Famous for its fly fishing, the Metolius is a cagey stream; it gives up its rainbows and native brown trout reluctantly. Well-fed lunkers lie below the Camp Sherman bridge, where waters are closed to fishing, waiting — seldom in vain — for bread crumbs from visitors.

Two major, long-time resorts bring people back year after year. Lake Creek Lodge is a great place for families, with a pond for the young and dinner served on the lodge's wide deck. The House on the Metolius, high above a gorge, draws anglers from all over the country; its view of Mount Jefferson above the curling river is one of the finest in Oregon.

When is the best time to visit the Metolius? Come in spring and you'll decide spring is the best season. Spring comes late in this 3000-foot valley. Not until April and May will the small meadows turn yellow with a million buttercups. Serviceberry brightens the woods with snowy blossoms, and drifts of forget-me-nots, their roots at the edge of the stream, copy the color of the sky.

Spring winds murmur in the tall ponderosa pines. The wren trills at one possible nest after another waiting for his flighty wife, and those beguiling clowns of the forest, the golden-mantled ground squirrels, leap across the grass once more.

But summer makes the forest really come alive. The Steller's jay is his most raucous, the kingfisher watches from a high branch above the river, and the water ouzel bounces on the wet rocks, disappearing under the swift current for startlingly long minutes. The ground squirrels grow rotund on an inevitable diet of peanuts from human admirers. The summer stretches long and hot; in the lazy evenings, night hawks swoop in wild grace above the stream. And by late June or early July the does will be seen with their freckled fawns on wobbly legs. Can any season beat summer?

Yet soon there's a quieter time. The serviceberry leaves are yellow, and the wild hawthorns along the stream turn rusty red. The winds are on holiday, and time sets a slower pace. Then you're sure that Indian summer on into autumn, as the lavender asters pop up beside the river path, is the loveliest. Now only manmade sounds — cracks from a deer rifle — shatter the peace, and you murmur, "I hope he missed — I hope he missed."

But autumn is too beautiful to last. Soon the nights are astonishingly cold, and by early November the tiny needles of the tamaracks have fallen softly like yellow snow, symbolic perhaps of what is to come. The nervous winds return, blowing down withered pine

A pampered doe seems to ask, "Where is everybody?" when human friends have fled the snows.

needles in a slanting brown rain. Then one morning the muffled silence signals the arrival of the first snow. Alder branches, ice-encased, lean stiffly above the water, and nothing moves across the white forest floor. The squirrels, obese after the summer's provender, are asleep in their cozy quarters underground, and the deer, what is left of them, their once tawny coats gone the gray of wet stone, stand imperiously at doorways where any people are still around. "Where is everybody?" they seem to ask. Even the jay, still here, is silent, his flight a flash of indigo above this suddenly white world. A cold world, too. And in this hushed landscape, no tree accepts its burden of snow with more grace than the ponderosa pine, its long needles agleam first with silver, then gold, as they catch the light of a shivery sun. So winter is special, too, and for skiers, pure joy.

SISTERS:
Poker Chips Built the Hotel

At the edge of town, clouds hide the peaks of the Three Sisters and, at left, Broken Top.

No town ever had a grander setting than Sisters. At the foot of that triumvirate of mountains called the Three Sisters, it is like a stage set, the gleaming peaks providing a backdrop across the broad meadows. At the west end of town, the Old McKenzie Highway and U.S. 20 funnel together out of the ponderosa pines into the main street, Cascade Avenue. Across Squaw Creek at the other end of town, the highway forks east to Redmond and southeast to Bend, and the juniper and sagebrush begin.

For years a sleepy lumber town, its inhabitants mostly loggers, Sisters maintained a static population of approximately 600 people. It is hardly larger now — some 700 at the last official count — but what a different place!

"They've ruined it," an old-timer moans. "It's just a tourist town now."

But ten miles northwest, at Black Butte Ranch, condominium and second-home owners exclaim, "Don't you just love Sisters?"

Sisters was a sleepy town, but today? Well, that depends on the season. All summer there are parking problems, and in early June, when the rodeo is on — that "biggest little show in the world" — the general feeling is, "Well, hell, you gotta celebrate sometime!" But come the snows, the town closes at least one eye.

A group of loyal pioneers rarin' to take care of some unruly native Americans was more or less responsible for the beginnings of Sisters. The First Oregon Volunteer Infantry came over from the Willamette Valley in what was undoubtedly the chilly winter of 1865-66 and camped on Squaw Creek. Their commanding officer called the place Camp Polk after his home county. Ten years later the camp had acquired a post office, but in 1888 it seemed practical to move the office to a new location on Squaw Creek about three miles to the southwest. The former Camp Polk settlers renamed their new community Sisters, but it took another thirteen years before a plan for a town site was recorded.

The name came naturally — what else but Sisters when those three mountain siblings stood close guard over the town? Some pious pioneers had called the peaks, which made helpful landmarks for wagon trains, Mount Faith, Mount Hope, and Mount Charity. But in time they became simply North Sister, 10,085 feet high and geologically the oldest and most deeply eroded; Middle Sister, at 10,047 feet; and South Sister, the highest, at 10,358 feet, its cone also most smoothly rounded.

Almost a century old now, Sisters had had little reason through the years to change its personality. Bend and Redmond, each about twenty miles distant, were central Oregon's cities. But when the beautiful old black-angus ranch that had belonged to the Howard Morgan family became Black Butte Ranch, the resort, with a grand contemporary lodge, a sweep of green golf course, and a manmade lake, Sisters suddenly became Black Butte's metropolis. People poured in to build around the edges of the marshy meadow at the foot of Black Butte, and Sisters in turn became a shopping town.

Shopping in Sisters used to consist of having a milkshake at the drugstore, which was and still is the liquor store as well; getting supplies at Pete Leithauser's grocery; and probably stopping for a hamburger at the restaurant called the Gallery. Today, modern shops, boutiques, and antique stores line Cascade Avenue. Behind the Gallery on Hood Street is a mall called the Gallery Annex; a bevy of small shops crowds Elm Street, and new banks and real estate offices have opened all over town. You may well hear some Portlander remark, "I love to come over here to shop." That's 150 miles, mind you.

The shops carry toys and quilts, copper pots and stained glass, health foods and hand-tailored sports clothes, reproductions of antiques and imported wines, and collectables and other antiques for which the term is sometimes a trifle euphemistic.

Nobody used to try to make Sisters anything but what it was. Now wooden false fronts and rustic signs try hard to give the town a frontier flavor. Still, the incongruities are entertaining. Drop into the unpretentious Ranch House on Hood Street for a sandwich — you'll be able to pick up a nice sixty-dollar bottle of German Rhine wine there.

There are certain places not to miss while visiting Sisters, and in the summer you'll have lots of company, including tourists coming through by camper, car, or van, visitors from the Willamette Valley, and always those faithful Black Butte shoppers.

The Elegant Dromedary on Elm Street has among its home furnishings some exotic Spanish perfumes and soaps, some unusually attractive Japanese pottery, and a fine collection of vinegars, mustards, chutneys, and jams such as black currant with navy rum.

The Stitchin' Post is a delight; it was one of the first shops to open a few years back when the new look came to Sisters. What with its prints and ribbons, its tapes and trimmings, owner Jean Wells calls it a "fantasy of cottons." The shop specializes in quilts. Indeed, the entire town is transformed into a quilt show in early June as the Stitchin' Post hangs some 200 quilts outdoors all over the place. Some are for sale; others — sometimes ones patiently stitched by pioneers — are simply to be admired. Distaff runners "from eight to eighty" start the quilt-show day with a three-mile run. A special quilt is raffled off, and lectures and workshops are also part of the program.

Sampling these and other shops is easy because everything lies within a few blocks. Paintings, pottery, and sculpture are exhibited on two floors at the Art Merchant Gallery; ladies' sportswear tailoring is available at Bernhard's; and charming, hand-twisted pine-needle baskets and coasters are a specialty at Memories, a tiny antique shop. Plum Pretty, the Paper Place, and half a dozen other stores are fun for browsing at the Gallery Annex, and you'll find

A little this, a little that, all old, are displayed in the Sisters Hotel window.

wooden nickels — for a dime — at the Dime Store. For oldies, try the Sisters Country Antiques; the old Sisters Hotel, an antique in its own right, has a tremendous collection, too.

Ah, the hotel. The two-story frame building was put up in 1914, though the small shop next door, built six years earlier, is said to have been the town's first hostelry. A source of funds came conveniently to early-day Sisters, it seems, when a young Englishman was sent by his family to America's burgeoning West. A Sisters resident told the story of how his late uncle had been a card shark. The Englishman liked poker, and apparently so did most everyone else in Sisters, for games were a nightly routine. Uncle, according to the Sisters raconteur, had a marked deck, but it never occurred to the Englishman "that a gentleman would cheat at cards." Eventually the poker shark built the hotel. His wife ran the dining room, to which loggers came from some distance, for the hearty dinners were said to be the best around.

The old hotel used to have an authoritative look. On both the front and side-street side the name Sisters Hotel was spelled in bold, black letters followed by a bold, black period. That big, black dot leant a certain no-nonsense finality to the structure.

During the 1970s, when the hotel had long stood idle, ten Portland business entrepreneurs who called themselves the Cosmic Cowboys bought the old building. The Cowboys had some grand plans. They started by repainting the building, adding an attractive balcony in front, and relettering the name, sans the period. One missed it somehow. They renovated the interior, papered the ten bedrooms with pretty prints, and covered the brass beds with handmade quilts. The new hotel was supposed to cater to skiers and was to feature a special room in which skiers could work on their equipment. But the Cowboys' dream was never quite translated into reality. The group sold the building, but the present owners promise that one day it will open again as a fine hostelry.

The Gallery is a good place for simple, hearty, well-cooked food, and it is an interesting place to visit because of the exceptional paintings of local landscapes and of Indians done by the late local artist Ray Eyerly. Before he died, his work had become famous throughout the region.

Your choice, beer with your sandwich or an imported vintage.

The sandwiches are superior at both the Ranch House Deli and the Depot Deli — at either place you may eat them indoors or out, or buy them "to go." And the pizzas at Papandrea's are said to be the best in Oregon. "A stranger," says Papandrea, "is a good friend we haven't met."

If you want very special fare, however, drive on to Redmond.

LA CIGALE:
A Touch of Elegance

A French restaurant in the middle of a lumber town where hamburgers and barbecued steaks are the popular fare? But there it is, plumb in the center of downtown Redmond in the old Redmond Hotel. La Cigale surprises diners by simply being where it is.

The hotel has been nicely refurbished, and in the high-ceilinged restaurant off the lobby, Persian rugs hang on the walls. A samovar rests in the window, Mozart fills the air, and the service is quiet and solicitous.

Ebullient chef Bruce Livingston, tall and bearded, studied the artistry of French cuisine in Paris. In the crowded kitchen of a Parisian restaurant, where he was a *stagier* — a step above apprentice — he heard his assistants saying that "the American is too big." But in La Cigale's ample kitchen, Livingston is doing what he likes best: preparing dishes that are as attractive as they are delicious. His cooking reflects the current trend back to basic French methods, such as those of the nineteenth century's great chef, Escoffier, avoiding the calorie-ridden, rich sauces and heavy dishes of haute cuisine. Livingston's first rule is that his meats, fish, and vegetables must be fresh, and so La Cigale's menus follow the seasons.

You may be sure that the *poisson en papillote* will not have been long out of the sea. The *poulet roti aux herbes* is a whole broiler cooked with a white cheese made from ricotta cheese, yogurt, and crushed herbs. The steak *au poivre* is a filet mignon pressed with green and black peppercorns. Each dinner begins with dainty puff-pastry hors d'oeuvres, and the liqueur-flavored ice creams are always served in *une tulipe,* a delicate, meringuelike tulip cup.

The restaurant's name — The Grasshopper — comes from a favorite French poem of the owner, whose feeling about how food should be prepared is noted on the menu in a quotation from Fernand Point: "If the divine creator has taken pains to give us delicious and exquisite things to eat, the least we can do is prepare them well and serve them with ceremony."

5
East Where the West Begins

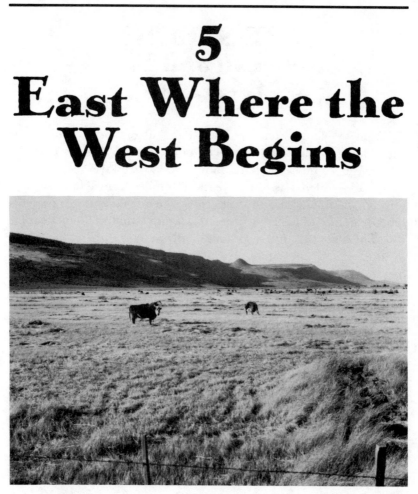

The Jackass Mountains rim the Blitzen Valley on the west.

"East is East and West is West, and never the twain shall meet." But they meet in eastern Oregon, which is where you go to find the West. The land of the ten-gallon hat and the high-heeled boot, of the eerie howl of the coyote at midnight, of what seems to be a million miles of sagebrush, is all east of the Cascades. Good roads get you there, but you may never want to come back.

THE STEENS:
Sagebrush and Turkey Buzzards

It was by "looks" that the late Reub Long, rancher and writer extraordinary, measured distances on the eastern Oregon plateau. "Well," he would say, "that's about two looks away."

It is a lot of looks as you drive the 130 miles from Bend to Burns through an infinity of sagebrush. It used to be that a wind-rain-and-time-demolished cabin or tattered windmill told of homesteaders who had come here full of promise, only to have the dry, hot winds of summer and the snows of winter destroy their crops and their hopes. Reminders are rare now, and rare the occasional irrigated field, until you reach the neighboring towns of Hines and Burns. Rare they are there, too, for these are lumber towns.

Better stop at Brothers for a break in the mesmerizing miles. Brothers? You guessed it. A group of brothers started the village in the teens of the century, and it just went on being called that. By recent count its population numbered thirty-two. Brothers has a scatter of houses, a bright red schoolhouse planted beside the highway, and a post office in one corner of a small cafe. The cafe is open from 6:00 a.m. to 9:00 p.m.; its sweet rolls are plump and fresh, the coffee a good dark brown.

Our destination is Frenchglen, that tiny outpost deep in Harney County's some 10,000 square miles. Brothers is something of a metropolis compared to Frenchglen. If you ask how to get there when you've reached Burns, you're likely to be told, "Maps ain't always so good — jest follow the telephone lines and you can't get lost." But there's no need. Simply leave U.S. 20 at Burns, follow State Highway 78 through town, and turn south onto State 205 for the fifty-nine miles to Frenchglen. It is fine paved highway all the way, with that endless ridge of mountain called the Steens on the horizon ahead. Almost as soon as you leave Burns, you'll be driving through the green of marsh country. Suddenly birds are everywhere, a curlew scolding from a fence post.

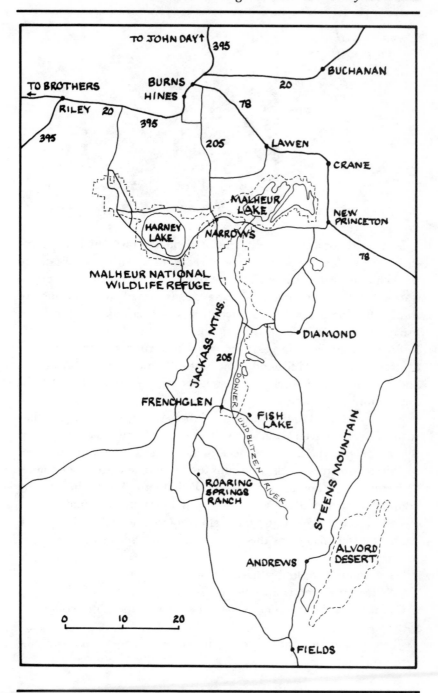

Aside from the hotel, the post office and general store is the busiest place in Frenchglen.

Soon, without any warning, you find yourself on Frenchglen's one short street. Along it are two or three houses, an attractive white schoolhouse with a large bell in the belfry, a general store, a service station, and a small hotel. The hamlet is famed for a number of things: for the dramatic days when it was headquarters for Peter French's vast cattle empire; for the Malheur National Wildlife Refuge, the nation's largest; for the wildly rugged Steens; for the obstreperous native redband trout in the Donner and Blitzen River; and for the little Frenchglen Hotel, where the service is old-fashioned family-style and the food contemporary gourmet.

Frenchglen used to have a sign on its one street, the highway, that read "This is Heaven, Don't drive like Hell." It must be heaven for the few people who live here, because no one seems to want to leave, including Malena Konek, who runs the Frenchglen Hotel. The hotel operator was a law student in the Willamette Valley before she adopted Frenchglen. Now she not only manages the small, state-owned hostelry, dreaming up its tempting menus and cooking up a storm, but she also owns the general store and serves as local postmaster.

"How many people live here?" you ask.

"Well, that depends on how you figure it."

Counting on her fingers, one of the girls at the hotel comes up with ten.

"Ten in summer, that is. Eight in winter. There aren't any jobs here in winter."

If you count the ranchers in a fifty-mile radius and the people who run the trailer camp at the foot of the Steens, you see where the village's forty registered voters come from.

The hotel's eight bedrooms are just big enough for the beds — nicely quilted and comfortable — and you. Facilities, European coachhouse style, are across the hall. Luxury is not a feature here, but hospitality is. "Laid back" is what the young might call it.

You'll dine at one of the two long tables on one side of the lobby. More like a living room, the lobby also has an old upright piano, some large, old lounge chairs, and always books on the table. Come here in autumn and the conversation may go something like this.

"Your first time here?" you ask the woman in a Harris tweed jacket and elegant boots.

"Oh, no. I always come in October to see the birds." These would be the thousands of geese and ducks on their fall migration across the Pacific Flyway.

Hunters come in the fall, too, after mule deer and elk, and in summer, fishermen head for the lakes on the Steens and for the feisty trout in the Donner and Blitzen — usually just called the

*Frenchglen Hotel's eight rooms often accommodate
more people than Frenchglen has residents.*

Blitzen. But what of the man who says he doesn't like hunting, doesn't like fishing, and isn't interested in bird watching?

"Then why are you here?"

"Because I hadn't ever been here."

Hikers, back from a strenuous climb on the Steens, come for dinner, but they will be camping over at Page Spring Campground at the foot of the mountain.

So the white-painted inn, Frenchglen's hotel since the teens and now nearly hidden by the surrounding poplars, has a steady clientele. Write ahead for reservations — for rooms, dinner, or both — to Malena Konek, Frenchglen Hotel, Frenchglen, Oregon 97736, or telephone (503) 493-2526.

The name Frenchglen comes from Peter French and his California partner in the French-Glenn Livestock Company, Dr. Hugh Glenn. With six Mexican vaqueros, French drove 1200 cattle from Sacramento to Oregon in 1872 and started an empire. He took a look at the Blitzen Valley, hemmed by the Steens on the southeast and the Jackass Mountains on the west, and decided it should be his. For twenty-five years it was.

French married Glenn's city-loving daughter and brought her to the P Ranch, named, not for Peter, but for a man named Porter, whose squatter's rights French quickly acquired. His wife failed to appreciate the far horizons below the Steens and eventually divorced him and returned to California. But French stayed on to build a multimillion-dollar fortune in the valley he loved.

The grass grew so high then they say a man on horseback could get lost from view. It was paradise for a cattleman, and Pete French was a shrewd one. One by one he bought out the local ranchers, and as settlers pushed in regardless, he pushed them out. On 132,000 acres of his own and on adjacent public domain he ran 45,000 cattle. To his vaqueros French was a hero; to his rivals he was a tough hombre — and to one rival in particular his power became intolerable.

Many stories have been written about French's death, but the most accurate is probably the one written by John Scharff in the March 1982 issue of *Desert Trails,* the monthly magazine published in Burns. Scharff records the story told to him in August 1935 by

Emanuel Clark, a man who was there on the day before Christmas, 1897, when Edward Oliver shot French off his horse.

French, Scharff tells, was in the lead as he and Clark were moving a herd from one field to another. Clark saw Oliver "ride out of a slough toward French" and charge him, "knocking French's horse to its knees." French struck Oliver's horse, and, writes Scharff, "Oliver then checked his horse and pulled a pistol. Pete whirled his horse and started riding away from Oliver at an angle, looking back. Oliver fired, hitting Pete at the butt of the right ear near the temple. Pete immediately fell from his horse. Emanuel Clark was the first man to reach Pete and Pete died just as Dave arrived without speaking."

It was Dave, then — David Crow — Scharff continues, who set off at once by horseback to rush the news to Winnemucca to be telegraphed from there to the family home in Willows, California. Crow changed horses nine times along the way, stopped just twice for a 2½-hour sleep each time, and made it to Winnemucca in forty-eight hours.

"This," Scharff says, "is perhaps one of the most strenuous and spectacular rides ever made in this part of the country."

Frontier justice was questionable. Oliver immediately reported the murder, hired a skillful attorney from Portland, and after an emotional trial was quickly acquitted.

Pete French's empire soon fell apart, but its bogs and fields, its river, springs, and creeks, would become, in time, the larger part of the great Malheur National Wildlife Refuge, where in spring and fall the heavens are filled with birds.

MALHEUR REFUGE:
Playing Tag with a Hawk

Visit the attractive brick headquarters at the northern end of the preserve before you begin exploring. You may want to stop here on your way from Burns — the refuge is thirty-two miles south of Burns,

*When it all be-
longed to him,
Pete French used
to train his horses
in this round barn
now on Malheur
Refuge.*

including the half dozen miles on the road leading in from the highway.

At headquarters you will be given a forty-two-mile auto-tour map of the entire area, with alternate routes depending on what you want to see. If you want help in identifying birds in the refuge, be sure to visit the museum here. It is open every day from 6:00 a.m. to 9:00 p.m. and is free.

Gravel roads throughout the refuge, plenty dusty in summer, are open all year when weather permits. Along one is Pete French's famous round barn, a curious relic, its shingled roof like a huge Chinese coolie's hat. Within the wooden walls is a circular rock wall, and inside that, supporting the barn, a circle of thick, peeled tree trunks, with one great cedar bole at the center. French used the barn for saddle training of wild horses.

This wild country seems a million miles from anywhere, with its meadow grasses tinged lavender blue where the lupine blooms in summer and dark where basalt juts out in rugged outcroppings. A volcanic area called Diamond Craters has been described as looking like a "thin, rocky pancake with a few bumps." Those bumps, how-ever — those domes and craters and lava flows — mean a lot to geolo-gists, and supplied with a folder from headquarters, you may well turn into an amateur one yourself.

Part of the tour road edges broad Malheur Lake, a great, shallow marsh that expands and shrinks with the season. It sometimes spills through the Narrows into Harney Lake; in winter it becomes a sheet of ice. Into the flooded meadow in spring come multitudes of snow

On the refuge patrol road, willow clumps hide the water where the coots and mallards bob.

geese, Canada geese, whistling swans, ducks, and sandhill cranes. From mid-March into April, 125,000 waterfowl will occupy the refuge, and from 80,000 to 90,000 again in autumn. By May most of the migrants will have departed, but numerous Canada geese and sandhill cranes will be building nests to settle down and raise a family.

It is lovely here in September and October, when Indian summer settles across the valley — a lazy, soporific time. Take the patrol road and a hawk may well play tag with you, flying just ahead from one telephone pole to the next. The road beside the canal is edged with willow hedges so dense that you have to search for openings from which to spy the mallards and coots that bob on the water.

Magpies wing away on the soft breeze, and kingfishers watch the water from the highest willow branches. A whir in the brush, and a ring-neck pheasant rises swiftly and is gone before you've had more than a glimpse. Sometimes an owl discovers you as you discover him, half-asleep on a snag. Slowly he turns his head 180 degrees to decide if you are a hazard in his life or merely an interruption. If you are very lucky, you may even see a pair of trumpeter swans gliding across the quiet water of a small pond, lifting their long, graceful necks in unison in a rite the rangers call pair bonding. They do the same thing during courting time in the spring, and they mate for life. Sometimes their resonant voices echo across refuge ponds, making a sound that Michael Harwood, writing about swans for *Audubon,* said was like "thin, ancient horns." The trumpeters are permanent residents of the refuge.

Vultures gather on a tall tower at the old P Ranch in early morning and evening twilight conferences.

You will have no trouble identifying the turkey buzzards — the vultures. Go over to the P Ranch, about a mile from the Frenchglen Hotel, to see them gather on the tall observation tower there. Just after sunup these black scavengers perch on the tower's steel rungs, often spreading their wings wide as if to soak up the sun. Then a leader takes off toward the Steens, and one by one the others follow.

At twilight the buzzards meet again on the tower in noisy conference. Perhaps they're discussing the day's work, or, like fishermen, competing to tell the tallest tale. As the sun goes down they disappear into the leafy cottonwoods to roost for the night. The Steens is their hunting ground, and, curiously, they arrive here each spring, their brown-headed young in tow, nearly always on March 19 with almost the precision of the swallows at Capistrano.

THE MOUNTAIN:
Up and Up to the Top

Set aside a full day to take the seventy-mile loop trip over Steens Mountain — a slow and dusty trip, but wonderful. You'll want to stop often. From Page Spring Campground, the road winds up to the summit, then swings back down to Highway 205, ten miles south of Frenchglen.

"The weather," says the Bureau of Land Management sign at the foot of the mountain, "can change in a few minutes"; so be wary of darkening skies. The road seldom opens before July.

No pointed spire pierces the sky from the Steens. For thirty miles the undulating crest of this great fault-block mountain simply grows higher and higher until it has reached some 9700 feet, then tapers off gradually again. From the 4000-foot valley floor, its western slopes ascend gradually enough, but its eastern side plummets for a vertical mile to the wide-stretching Alvord Desert.

Signs mark the changing elevation as the road climbs, sometimes in steep inclines, again in roller-coaster dips, with swirling plumes of dust behind you. Tall sage covers the slopes at first. Then junipers appear, and by 6500 feet aspen that higher still will fill the upper slopes of great ravines, their quaking leaves a soft, fresh green in July and a mass of gold come October.

By late July, spring's wildflowers — buttercups, Indian paintbrush, mimulus, lupine, shooting stars, and a thousand others, all the flowers that you enjoyed at lower elevations in May — carpet the slopes on the way to the barren, rocky summit. At 8000 feet sub-alpine grass has replaced them.

It can be a dusty ride up the Steens, but it's worth it.

In his book *North with the Spring,* naturalist Edwin Way Teale explains how, "as spring goes on and on, it also goes up and up." Botanists, he says, calculating changes in vegetation at different levels, say that a climb of 1000 feet up a mountain "is equal to a northward journey of 600 miles."

As far as plants go, then, an ascent to the top of the Steens, from 4000 feet in the valley to approximately 9700 feet, would be the same as a trip of some 3000 miles northward. Where would that take you? Past the Arctic Circle to where?

Fish Lake, eighteen miles up the road from the valley, is the first water you encounter; it is a popular place with campers and fishermen. As you climb higher, alpine meadows and tiny, blue pothole lakes appear, some with water lilies and miniature islands of grass. As you continue to follow the dusty road, cirques choked with aspen head great canyons — glacier-dug gorges — with always a hawk flying over, perhaps a prairie falcon, riding the wind currents, its slight shadow momentarily darkening the gleam of aspen on the side of a chasm or darkening the winding ribbon of stream at the bottom. Snow lies in the swale at the head of Little Blitzen Gorge, and the canyons grow deeper. Soon there are no trees, but everywhere grass of a tarnished green gold like antique velvet.

A couple of vultures fly up from some secret find in the brush — ugly critters. You're a long way from your tower, fellas.

The sign reads "9500 feet," and at the East Rim View is that sudden, stunning expanse — dessicated lava walls and the salty-looking desert a sheer mile below. The twenty-three-mile ride up has been a preview of the return trip: more lakes, more U-shaped, scooped-out cuts in the mountainside, back down through the mountain's changing life zones to the wildflowers, and eventually, a touch reluctantly, to the paved road again. Perhaps a little let down to be back from the heights, but very much ready for dinner!

Hikers are the ones who come to know the mountain intimately, to know its most rugged aspects and its most beautiful. The very names of their camps — Wet Blanket Meadow, for example — suggest a hardy closeness to the heart of the mountain. Wary of its dangers, but accustomed to them, hikers share the philosophy of the valley cowpoke who remarked, "Sure there are rattlers around, but rattlers are a friendly enemy. They always warn you before they strike, and that's more than some people do."

The Desert Trail Association, headquartered in Burns, organizes hikes and nature walks from spring through fall in the Steens country, a trip to watch the spring mating dance, or "strut," of the sage grouse, and a ten-day hike up the Steens from 4400 to 9700 feet, exploring gorges along the way. Another offering is a four-day backpack trip through the Pueblo Mountains over the completed twenty-two-mile section of the Desert Trail between Fields, fifty-two miles south of Frenchglen, and Denio, Nevada. The trail is part of a statewide network of interconnecting trails being developed by the Park and Recreation Division of the State Department of Transportation and citizen groups.

An extension of the Desert Trail eventually will cross Steens Mountain, with another branch edging the Alvord Desert. A fold-up map and description of the finished segment is available for a nominal fee by writing to the Desert Trail Association, P.O. Box 589, Burns, Oregon 97720.

THE JOHN DAY COUNTRY: Cows on the Road, Ghosts in the Hills

John Day left his name all over Oregon. A town, two rivers, a dam on the Columbia, and a national monument all carry the name of this hunter-explorer who came west with John Jacob Astor's overlanders — the Wilson Price Hunt expedition — in 1811. Curiously enough, Day's wanderings never took him into that fascinating land of prehistoric fossils in the John Day Valley. But his experiences not far from where the John Day River empties into the Columbia were bizarre enough for his name to be remembered throughout the region.

Washington Irving, in his romantic account *Astoria,* says of John Day at the time of the expedition: "He was about forty years of age, six feet two inches high, straight as an Indian; with an elastic step as if he trod on springs, and a handsome, open, manly countenance." It was Day's "boast," Irving adds, "that in his younger days nothing could hurt or daunt him; but he had 'lived too fast' and injured his constitution by his excesses."

This may be partly why Day became so exhausted on the trek to the Pacific that he fell behind the rest of the group. Ramsay Crooks stayed with him, and, helped by hospitable Indians, the two men later started toward the Pacific again. But luck was against them. On the banks of the Columbia, Indians attacked, took their weapons, their food, their clothes, and left them naked on the banks of the river in the chill winds of early spring.

In his *General History of Oregon,* Charles H. Carey tells the story of how an old Indian, close to starvation himself, took the men in, fed them, and gave them skins to wear. The two men were about to start out again, this time toward the east in hopes of reaching Missouri, when David Stuart and his party, traveling down-river by canoe from Astor's trading post in the Okanagan, heard a hail in English from the shore. Soon Day and Crooks were in the canoes headed downstream for Astoria, but not before Stuart had outfitted the old Indian with clothes.

Later, when Day's mind snapped, the hardships he had known on this journey were thought to have been the cause, but that is another tale.

To paleontologists, the John Day country is a treasure-trove of fossilized bones of elephants and tiny camels, rhinoceroses and tapirs, cud-chewing oreodonts and saber-toothed cats. To ranchers it means vast acres of pasture for beefstock, and to travelers it is a new world to explore, including the prehistory told by its fossils, somnolent small towns in which to browse, and ghost towns where gold, like a human-attracting magnet, once drew thousands of men armed with picks, axes, and high hopes.

John Day, seventy miles north of Burns where U.S. Highways 26 and 395 meet, is a cow town, friendly as cow towns always are, and easy-paced. The Malheur National Forest lies within a few miles north, south, and east, so there's a pleasant choice of pine-shaded

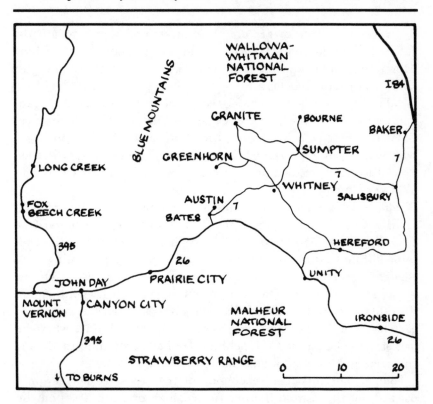

campgrounds, as well as a chunk of wilderness in the Strawberry Range just to the southeast. The National Forest office is located in the middle of town.

John Day has comfortable accommodations, including Dreamer's Lodge, which sits quietly off the main street. Burton's is a good place for dinner, and the Antique Cafe — "Antique" because of the fine antique store upstairs — is the spot for breakfast.

An eavesdropper overhears a dialoque from one of the cafe's booths:

"Since when have you seen a menu offering milk toast?"

"Milk toast? What's that?"

"You know, graveyard stew."

"Oh, sure. I can't remember when before."

It is something of an adventure in John Day simply to drive up the curling road to the airport, which sits on a mesa squarely above the town — a fine place to get oriented. Stretching westward are the folded hills of the John Day River Valley, to the northeast the Blue Mountains, and below, the pretty town with its spired churches. Just over 2000 people live here.

John Day got its start in 1862, when gold was discovered in Canyon Creek. This is the little creek that bubbles along beside the road in Canyon City, which is hardly a mile south of John Day on Highway 395. When gold washed down the brook, and whiskey washed down the gullets of the miners, the names were Whiskey Creek and Whiskey Gulch.

The late Herman Oliver wrote a warm and entertaining book, *Gold and Cattle Country,* in which he tells of the man who took the first nuggets out of Whiskey Gulch. William C. Aldred, with other miners from California, was on his way to the Idaho diggings. He thought the creek a likely prospect, and he waded across, up to his waist in the cold water. But, Oliver says, he had left his gold pan on the other side. So he took off his long johns, knotted the bottom of each leg, and filled the impromptu sacks with gravel. Back where he had started, he panned the pebbles. He had, according to Oliver, collected $4.50 worth of gold in his dripping woollies.

Soon prospectors lined each side of the creek. After they had panned out the easy stuff, they turned high-pressure hoses on the hillsides, and later, about the turn of the century, miners gouged out the meadows with dredges. Estimates vary widely as to how much gold was produced in the area, but its value ran well into the millions.

At least 5000 miners crowded into the camp at Whiskey Gulch after the 1862 gold discovery. Freight wagons churned up the road, and three times a week pony-express riders galloped into town after a 225-mile dash from The Dalles. Echoes of the Civil War are also said to have sounded occasionally. One historian notes that when California miners hoisted the Confederate flag in the hills, Unionist Oregonians raced uphill and tore it down.

It was the suppression of his secessionist-leaning newspaper, the *Eugene City Democratic-Register,* that brought Joaquin Miller — who would become the "poet of the Sierras" — to Whiskey Gulch. Miller brought his wife, baby, and a band of cattle over Santiam

Pass and built a house in the hills above the camp. When Grant County was formed in 1864, with Canyon City as the county seat, Miller was elected its first judge. Now his small cabin, silvered with age and moved downhill, stands at one side of Grant County's Oliver Historical Museum on the highway in the center of Canyon City. Next to it is a two-cell jail, its small windows iron-barred.

The twelve-by-fourteen-foot jail originally was in the town of Greenhorn. Then one morning in 1963, there it was, sitting beside Miller's house in Canyon City. "Jailnapped," they say, and you will be told that Baker County's district attorney came over with a court order demanding its return, but local authorities told him that it could not be taken away — it was too wide to be hauled up the highway legally.

Nearly hidden under the branches of mountain ash now, the little jail looks as sturdy as it must have been when it was built in 1910. According to Miles Potter, in his *Oregon's Golden Years,* the man who built the jail was so proud of his handiwork that he went on a spree and ended as the jail's first prisoner.

The Greenhorn jail was jailnapped, it now sits beside Highway 395 in Canyon City.

It was even sturdier perhaps than one up in Condon, which certain old-timers insist moved off its foundation one night without any outside help. During a festive evening, they say, two men in their cups were thrown into the tiny hoosegow, each one convinced that he could do without the other. While the celebration went on, the two inmates slugged it out, and the story goes that the next morning the jail was still upright but in a new location.

Both of Canyon City's architectural relics have been fenced in, but when the museum is open, you may enter the gate and peer through the cabin's dusty windows at a realistic papier-mâché figure of Miller, with a long, white beard flowing down over a fringed buckskin jacket.

In the spacious museum, life is portrayed as it was in gold rush and homesteading days. You'll see farm furnishings and tools, a large collection of old guns, and an extensive display of rocks and mining paraphernalia. Although many of Canyon City's oldest buildings burned in a disastrous fire in 1937, some early landmarks are left, including St. Thomas' Episcopal Church, with its gleaming stained-glass windows, built in 1876. Services are still held here every Sunday morning.

Drive up the twisting road to the county cemetery above town. The "bad guys" were supposed to have been the first to be buried

A prospector, done in papier mâché, holds ore in his gold pan in the Oliver Historical Museum.

Gashes in the hills above Canyon City mark where miners washed out pay dirt with hydraulic hoses.

here. Herman Oliver, however, wrote that justice was so swift in Whiskey Gulch that the worst types avoided the gold camp. Many an elaborate old tombstone dates from the last decades of the nineteenth century. In spring, the only sound you may hear is the melancholy lament of a mourning dove, answered like an echo from the hills that roll away into the blue distance. Long gashes in the slopes above Canyon Creek still mark the paths where hydraulic hoses washed out pay dirt.

In Prairie City, fifteen miles to the northeast on Highway 26, the small De Witt Museum has preserved many of those huge metal tools that hydraulic mining required. The museum, on the main street, also contains a clutter of old books and pictures.

On your way to Prairie City, about six miles beyond John Day, watch for the Holliday Ranch on the north side of the highway. It is the Holliday herd that annually turns John Day back a century as cowboys drive several thousand head of cattle right up Main Street. Nobody minds, though; cars pull over, and the show goes on for several hours.

GOLDEN GHOSTS:
Only Tired Cabins Are Left

Some miner once had a pretty good cabin here in the Greenhorn suburbs.

Northeast into the Blue Mountains in the Wallowa-Whitman National Forest is a cluster of ghost towns — towns that were born of gold and that died as the gold died. Thousands of miners came up the Columbia River by steamer to The Dalles, then here by horse and mule pack. Sometimes a dilapidated two-story building, but more often tired cabins, their roofs sagging, doors aslant, and window panes missing, identify the sites of these once booming towns.

A few have a renewed summertime life as city-dwellers come for a bit of clean air, clear streams, and the touch of romance that surrounds a gold-rush ghost town. Modern prospectors also come to work the creeks with gold pan and sluice box.

The way to sample this country is along State Highway 7, the paved shortcut to Baker, then by the graded dirt and gravel roads that branch off it. Fourteen miles northeast of Prairie City, U.S. 26 meets Highway 7 at the Austin junction. A loop trip of approximately sixty-five miles from this point will take you to Whitney, Sumpter, Granite, and Greenhorn, with other locales and mines accessible if you want to make a longer trip.

Whitney is the first ghost town on the loop. Never a gold center, it was a busy community nevertheless, for it was the midway stop on the Sumpter Valley Railroad's eighty-mile, narrow-gauge line between Baker and Prairie City — the miners called the railroad the Stump Dodger because its roadbed was so rough. Lots of miners lived in Whitney during winters, when deep snows and temperatures down to -30°F closed the mines. Only a handful of steep-roofed houses and an old sawmill reflected in its log pond are reminiscent now of better days.

Sumpter, however, once one of the most rip-roaring of the lot, is still something of a town. About a hundred people live there in summer. Incorporated in 1890, Sumpter was the center for hard-rock mining, which developed some three decades after gold was discovered in the Powder River in 1862. During the early 1900s dredges scooped gold out of creek banks and meadows. The ugly ridges of rock and gravel along present-day roads tells that story.

In 1862, South Carolinians named the town Fort Sumter, and the name evolved over the years to Sumpter. Miles Potter, who has written so entertainingly of the era in *Oregon's Golden Years,* says that by 1900 the city's businesses included seven hotels, six restaurants, sixteen saloons, several general stores, two churches, two banks, five cigar stores, a cigar factory, a brewery, and an opera house! Then, in 1917, a tremendous fire destroyed the heart of the city. Amid today's reminders — an occasional brick foundation or wall — a scattering of new houses comprises the former boom town.

Granite, fifteen miles northwest of Sumpter, was quite a metropolis toward the end of the nineteenth century. Some say that 5000 persons lived in its hills. But as the gold dwindled, so did Granite, and the town is now listed as having just seventeen residents.

Not many years ago, only one man, the late Otis Ford, lived in Granite. Since the town had been incorporated in 1899, Ford, who liked to tell tongue-in-cheek stories, used to say that he was both mayor and the entire city council. He was quoted as saying that his administration was Republican.

A favorite tale about the hermit, possibly apocryphal, concerns a television interview with him. It seems there was a bit of rehearsing before Ford and the interviewer went on the air. Then the reporter asked, "How old are you?"

*A Greenhorn
facility padlocked
for the season.*

"Damnit," Granite's lone resident is said to have replied, "I've already told you four times!"

Greenhorn has its legends, too. The town's name comes from a nearby peak of green serpentine that resembles a horn. Potter explains how miners, calling it the Green-Horn, used it as a landmark. The two words eventually were combined, and now the local mountains that form a range within the Blues are known as the Greenhorn Mountains.

Inquire about the name, however, and you probably will be told — and whoever tells you will probably believe this — that a young greenhorn came tramping into Whiskey Gulch one day to ask where he could find some gold.

"A fur piece," he presumably was told. "Thataway."

And so the novice went thataway, and, of course — what else? — hit one of the area's richest deposits. Who knows now? Perhaps some rookie did just that. But the peak that looks like a horn stands tall and green in the Greenhorn Mountains.

At 6500 feet above sea level, Greenhorn is Oregon's highest and smallest incorporated town. Climb the steep road to the level spot where buildings once lined Main Street, and you may still find snow lying in the recesses as late as mid-June. Except for a bashed-in cabin at the edge of the ghost town, Greenhorn's few houses appear to be comparative newcomers. Miles Potter and his wife live in one of them during the summer. Potter is Greenhorn's elected mayor.

Poking around the forest-rimmed flat, you just might encounter another old-timer, Guy Miller, who wears a police badge and says he keeps an eye on the area for the sheriff.

"There's just the mayor and his wife and me up here," says Miller, who claims that he has lived in these parts, in a tent, for a quarter of a century.

"Any trouble up here now?"

"No trouble," Miller replies. "I just show 'em this," and he pats the holster that holds a .38, "and they go home."

In his book, Potter tells about how two stages a day used to swing up the mountain, and how, when the snow became too deep to get through, the driver would switch to skis, using a rope around his waist to tie himself to the harness.

In 1919 the mines closed, the miners left, and the post office closed its doors. Peace reigns in Greenhorn now, disturbed only by the rustling of wind in the pines. Perhaps it whispers of the gold some say is still deep down in the mountains called Blue, and that someday . . .

It's a lovely drive back to John Day with the snow-streaked Strawberry Range on the near southern horizon. You may well meet occasional cyclists, their gear neatly packed, who are with one of the

Crossing the continent by bike, this New York couple says, "There's a lot to Oregon." The Strawberry Range is in the background.

Bicentennial Association groups that cross the continent each year from Astoria to Williamsburg, Virginia. Highway 26 is their route across Oregon on the 4400-mile journey.

One couple riding slowly up the grade on fifteen-speed bikes stops to chat.

"I didn't know there was so much *to* Oregon," said Lydia Archer, out from Rochester, New York. "There's so much diversity, and all so beautiful."

"We've been two-and-a-half weeks coming from Astoria," said her husband, Stephen. "We're not trying for any records; we're just enjoying the scenery."

It's likely you'll want some of that milk toast when you get back to John Day.

FOSSILS:
In a Moonscape Land

The John Day Fossil Beds lie forty miles to the west of John Day. When you start in that direction through the tumbled hills of the John Day Valley and the cottonwood-shaded towns of Mount Vernon and Dayville, remember, about a mile and a half east of Mount Vernon, to look on the north side of the highway for a small stone building. It was built as a fort for a horse!

It seems that after the Civil War a Confederate Army captain rode west on an elegant black stallion named Mount Vernon. Apparently, everyone in the vicinity coveted that animal, particularly the local Indians. As it turned out, a rancher wanted the horse, and the captain wanted land; so they traded. But the horse kept disappearing, although it always reappeared after a few days. It seems that Mount Vernon was being encouraged to make the acquaintance of the mares among the Indians' mustangs.

Frustrated, the rancher built a stone stable with narrow slits in its thick walls just large enough for the butt of a rifle. Evidently, the little fort also aided neighboring ranchers, who were said to have

This was built as a fort to protect the stallion for which Mount Vernon was named.

crowded in with the horse during Indian troubles. Like John Day, the steed left his name around, for both the nearby butte and the town are called Mount Vernon. He really must have been a beauty!

Four miles west of Dayville, the John Day River turns abruptly north on its way to the Columbia. Suddenly it races through a narrow defile, with basalt cliffs 800 feet high on either side. The road follows the river. This is the famous Picture Gorge, named for the Indian pictographs now barely discernible.

Here U.S. 26 connects with State Highway 19, which wriggles north beside the river for some forty miles and then continues all the way to the Columbia River at Arlington. Take Highway 19 for the short distance out of the gorge and to the visitor center of the John Day Fossil Beds National Monument.

You are entering a moonscape land of strangely shaped buttes that have been deeply gouged out by erosion. They form a weird profile above the now calmly flowing river. Of ashen hue, and banded in pale shades of buff and green and rust — colors that look faded by the sun — the buttes have an eerie quality, even in the bright sunshine of a midsummer day.

In the various formations scattered throughout the monument's 14,000 acres, 40 million years are recorded in fossil deposits. As erosion uncovered thick layers of volcanic ash, the fossilized bones of prehistoric mammals and the clear imprints of leaves and seeds revealed that this now dry, sagebrush-covered landscape has evolved through eras of inland seas and lakes and subtropical climates. The park is divided into three sections where fossils from various epochs

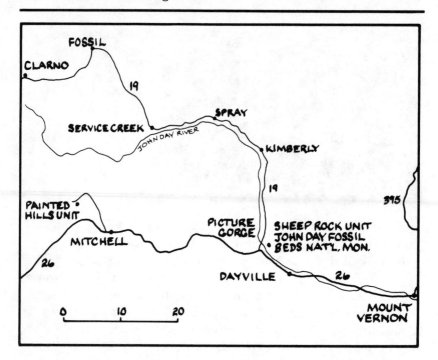

have been found: the John Day beds, the Painted Hills near Mitchell, and the Clarno deposits twenty miles west of the town of Fossil.

It was Thomas Condon, a minister who came from New York to The Dalles in 1852, who was responsible for acquainting scientists with the natural treasures here. A cavalry officer who had been in the John Day area with a group of Indian fighters brought a fossil specimen to Condon at The Dalles. Condon was as interested in the evolutionary story told in the earth as he was in his religion, and he found no conflict between the two.

Later Condon became the University of Oregon's first geology professor, but at this time he investigated the region himself and sent some fossilized teeth to Yale University. It was the start of studies that have been made here by scientists from all over the world. To preserve these rare resources, the state bought various tracts with exceptional deposits and made them into state parks, and in 1974 Congress established the national monument.

The visitor center is in the old Cant Ranch house, restored and shining white now, and surrounded by tree-shaded lawns with picnic tables for visitors. This is a great place for a quick course in geology and paleontology, for a fascinating glimpse into millions of years of changing life forms. So before you start exploring the trails, peruse the center's fossil specimens and read the charts tracing the different forms of plant and animal life on the geologic calendar.

Sheep Rock, with its tilting cap of dark basalt, lies just across the river from the center. Its name derives from the mountain sheep that used to be seen there. The nearby overlook provides explana-

From eroded slopes like these on Sheep Rock came fossils of prehistoric life.

tory signs, and two short trails lead from it to closer views. As you wander these dry pathways through the sagebrush, can you imagine how the land may have looked 25 million years ago, when deciduous trees like birch and oak grew here in a mild, moist climate? *Miohippus,* a small ancestor of the horse, grazed on meadowlands, and so did herds of oreodonts, which were similar in size to sheep.

Continue on down the road from the visitor center to Cathedral Rock, one of the most impressive of these fluted bluffs, its pallid slopes banded in pastel hues as though painted with a giant paintbrush. The butte is all that is left of an ancient landslide.

The Painted Hills are only a few miles off Highway 26 on the way to Bend, which is where you are headed. Clarno, some eighty miles to the northwest, is a rugged area of deeply eroded palisades. Fossils found there represent the dawn age of mammals in this part of the world. Forty million years ago small rhinos, giant dogs, and crocodiles lived in the region in a subtropical climate among palm and fig trees. If you detour to Clarno, remember that no water is available there, and watch out for snakes.

The twenty-five miles from the Picture Gorge to Mitchell, which is near the turnoff to the Painted Hills, make for a varied, back-country ride. Out of the canyon walls of the gorge, the road follows bubbling Mountain Creek at the foot of tumbled hills, with willow and cottonwood crowding the water's course and tall sage covering the hillsides. Then the route climbs high to wide views. As you come down one steeply curving hillside three miles before you reach Mitchell, watch for a small, inconspicuous, rock monument on the north side of the road.

As its inscription will tell you, the monument honors unflappable stage driver Henry H. Wheeler, who, on an autumn day in 1866, came jouncing down this hill behind his four-horse team. Wheeler had been carrying supplies from The Dalles to the miners in Whiskey Gulch for a couple of years. Indian encounters were nothing new to him, but this one was memorable.

Wheeler had only one passenger that day, a Wells Fargo Express agent, but he was carrying the mail and a variety of valuables, including $10,000 in currency. Without warning, a band of rifle-shooting Indians swooped down on the coach. A bullet went clean through both of Wheeler's cheeks, taking a piece of his jaw with it. Nevertheless, the feisty driver leapt out and unhitched his lead team while his passenger shot it out with the attackers. The men then jumped onto the horses, which had never been ridden before, and went careening down the hill.

After being bandaged up at a roadhouse down the way, Wheeler and the agent returned to what was left of the coach. It had been literally torn apart, the mail sacks ripped open, and the greenbacks blown about all over the place. The paper money obviously had held no interest for the Indians, but they had taken the leather off the coach's seats. Once sewn up, Wheeler continued his three-days-a-week service on the run through Indian country.

Somehow the little monument hardly seems adequate for stage driver Wheeler. Still, this is Wheeler County — they named the county after him.

Mitchell is worthy of a stop. It's like a western movie set, enhanced occasionally by a cattle drive along the adjoining highway. About 200 people live on the town's steep hillside above Bridge Creek in such apparent peace as to make it hard to picture the drama the place has known. Old men often sit chatting in the sun on the sidewalk of the town's curling main street. But in earlier years

An occasional cattle drive on the highway beside Mitchell
adds a bit of color to the sleepy town.

Mitchell, established in the 1860s as a station on The Dalles to Canyon City stage road, was virtually washed away by flood and cloudburst, and several times nearly burned up.

Bridge Creek, an innocuous-looking streamlet is tributary to the John Day. "Mild little Bridge Creek," comments Charles Mecartie, proprietor of the Little Pine Cafe. "A thunder storm and it's a raging torrent."

When the town acquired a post office in 1873, it was named for John H. Mitchell, at that time the United States senator from Oregon. The name was suggested by "Brawdie" Johnson, local blacksmith and the community's first postmaster.

Among the few items for sale in Mecartie's cafe is a delightful small book, *Glimpses of Wheeler County's Past,* edited by F. Smith Fussner. Among some hilarious tales is the one recalling an early day during the Canyon City gold rush when a freighter's "Mitchell" wagon — a vehicle popular then for its sturdiness — broke an axle about where Mitchell is now. Stymied, the freighter thought to sample the liquid cargo he was taking to the miners. Thus duly inspired, he set up shop on a bench made from a board off the wagon. Soon, from out the woods came customers, who went back to tell their compatriots. As long as the cargo lasted, his was a thriving business. Old-timers, according to the story, insisted that that was how Mitchell really got its name.

The Little Pine Cafe is a pleasant place to stop for an ice cream cone or a sandwich. It has some very nice prints of local landscapes on the walls, the work of central Oregon artist Mary Ross. And the general store is sheer discovery. It's a department store, hardware store, drugstore, and every other kind of store in one — it's fun to see if there's anything you can't find.

Three miles west of Mitchell, the Burnt Ranch Road follows Bridge Creek into the Painted Hills. You begin to see the hills quite soon. At six miles there's a grand view from an overlook, and a half-mile trail takes you to Painted Cove for a closer vantage point.

Barren, strange, and fascinating, these softly rounded hills rise in small to high domes. Some are rusty red; some are almost white; others look as if great scoops of cocoa had been poured over their tops; and nearly all are banded in buff, and pale green, and black.

Bands of rainbow hues seem to have been brushed across the folded buttes of the Painted Hills.

They are part of the John Day geologic formation, as are the dissimilar-looking shale rock buttes along the John Day River. During the Oligocene time 30 million years ago, ash spewing out of the earth in volcanic eruptions continued to spread eastward over this region until it lay a thousand feet thick. Then, for millions of years more, faulting and erosion gradually exposed the fossils that supply the clues to the region's prehistory. Quantities of leaf fossils found in the Painted Hills, for example, tell of trees that were ancestral to our current oaks and redwoods.

"Time has no divisions to mark its passage," wrote Thomas Mann, and you roll easily enough from an ancient world where oreodonts chewed contented cuds to the smooth, modern pavement heading west. It will take about an hour and a half to drive the eighty miles to Bend from the intersection of Burnt Ranch Road and the highway. How long would that be in geologic time — some unimaginably minute part of a second? On the way, the shining peaks of Oregon's Cascades grace the skyline once more.

INDEX